BICYCLES
UP
KILIMANJARO

Nicholas Crane
& Richard Crane

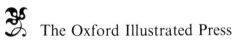 The Oxford Illustrated Press

© Nicholas Crane and Richard Crane, 1985

Printed in England by J. H. Haynes & Co. Limited,
Sparkford, Nr. Yeovil, Somerset.

ISBN 0 946609 27 6

The Oxford Illustrated Press Limited,
Sparkford, Nr. Yeovil, Somerset.

Published in North America by
Haynes Publications Inc,
859 Lawrence Drive, Newbury Park,
California 91320 USA.

Photographs by Peter Inglis
Illustrations by Catriona Hall

British Library Cataloguing in Publication Data

Crane, Nicholas
  Bicycles up Kilimanjaro
  1. Cycling—Tanzania—Kilimanjaro, Mount
  2. Kilimanjaro, Mount (Tanzania)—Description
  and travel
  I. Title   II. Crane, Richard, *1953*–
  916.78'26   DT449.K4
  ISBN 0–946609–27–6

Library of Congress Catalog Card Number

85–81436

Contents

For Jaro

Acknowledgements

With thanks to:
The Sunday Times, Kodak, Bluemels and Saracen, Karrimor, Black's, Berghaus, Sanctuary Mountain Equipment, Reebok Footwear, Chris Brasher, Aeroflot, Kenya Airways, Barrod Bennett, Kilimanjaro National Park, Nikon, K Shoes, *Bicycle Action,* Bike UK, Water Weights, John Lovesey, Richard Girling, Dr Mike Townend, Peter Roberts and innumerable friends.

Prologue

We'd left the road above the darkly sliding waters of Afon Anafon, standing on the pedals as hard-pumped tyres gripped tight damp turf; peering into the semi-darkness for the easiest line up the slope. Mist hung on the khaki folds of the hill like a dewy blanket on a still-sleeping tramp. We each had half a Mars Bar taped to our handlebars.

A thousand feet higher, the sun's rays were racing us up the rounded edge of Drum bringing a brilliant dawn as we neared the top. Clouds bubbled below. We rolled down to the next col and up the long grassy climb to Foel-fras, the 3,091-foot mountain which sits on the northern edge of Snowdonia. At the summit cairn—a careless pile set amid a field of scattered rocks—we pulled out the two pieces of paper that were our map. To save weight we'd torn the covers from sheets 65 and 66 of the Ordnance Survey 1:25,000 series, then ripped away all but the narrow strip of country along which we'd be travelling. A thin pencil line wandered across the contours reaching a pencil circle every few inches. There were fourteen circles; one for each mountain we had to visit. It was 5.20 am.

From Foel-fras the contours drop away to a gentle dip before Garnedd-uchaf. We started the stop-watch and rolled off, springing the bikes down between rocks, laughing with early-morning exhilaration. Marshy pools scattered into handfuls of twinkling droplets beneath our spinning wheels. Nobody else was on the mountains. The sun was climbing above the Conway valley; we were fit and the bikes felt light as down on the breeze.

Five peaks later, there was time at Ogwen Cottage for a jam sandwich and tin of rice pudding, then we winched ourselves up through the bogs at the base of Tryfan. Ahead, we had one of the hardest sections, for Tryfan is normally the preserve of rock-climbers rather than cyclists: the top part of the mountain is very steep and the bikes kept jamming in chimneys and threatening to topple us from narrow ledges. A rope of fiddling rock-gymnasts watched in silent astonishment as we overtook them with bicycles balanced on our heads.

Bristly Ridge was even more delicate, with airy traverses over huge drops. In a couple of places we had to stand on tip-toe and hang the bicycles from projecting rock spikes high above our heads, before climbing up ourselves. The sharp metal pedals proved to be painfully adroit at extracting blood from shins, and every now and again a suddenly swivelling handlebar would catch us on the temples with star-inducing impact.

There was some challenge to manoeuvring bikes over such unsuitable terrain, but with every yard of clambering the frustration increased. Crossing the first peaks of the Glyder range we found car-size blocks of rock thrown every which way. Sometime soon, we said to each other, we *must* be able to ride the wretched things.

At Glyder Fawr the gradients and terrain eased enough for us to throw the wheels to the ground and leap on saddles for some fast riding, racing down the slippery scree with stones and shale spitting from tyres that didn't quite want to hold. Past the little lake in the col, then, with aching legs a doomed attempt to ride up the inexorably steepening grassy side of Y Garn. Even our super-low gear couldn't manage to get us more than half-way up.

The long ridge that scythes north from Y Garn fell in a blur of numb effort. Communication between the two of us narrowed to snatched glances to check the other hadn't dropped over the edge, and the occasional shouted warning about tricky rocks and jumps. We juggled our wheels along the foot-wide track that curls around towards Elidir Fawr, knowing that after this peak, we just had the Snowdon range to tackle. We turned our backs on the cairn, setting our sights on a distant stream glimmering in the early-afternoon sunshine a thousand feet below, then flew down over grass tussocks, sliding round rocks; zig-zagging down and down with legs flexing on wildly bouncing pedals and aching arms hanging on for dear life to bucking handlebars.

Reaching the road proved to be an excuse for uncorking some high-octane inter-cousin competition and we tore wordlessly up Llanberis Pass, racing each other for the top. It was a grim sweat-lathered duel fuelled by pig-headedness rather than available energy. Three miles later, dizzy with dehydration, and in elaborately disguised states of near collapse, we reached Pen Y Pass, grabbed another sandwich and chased up the rocky path to the foot of Snowdon.

We chose the Crib Goch route, because it would be the quickest. Crib Goch is a precipitous ridge, in places just a few inches wide, with heart-stopping drops on each side. It was the final and most difficult hurdle and we crossed one memorable slab with toes on a tiny lip of rock and fingers hooked over the top of the ridge; bikes hanging delicately from one shoulder. At 7.36 pm we reached the top of Snowdon.

A soft sun dipped towards Anglesey. What, we wondered, could next be done on mountainbikes? We slotted the bikes' tyres into the central rack of the Snowdon railway, put our feet on the rails and accelerated off towards the long cool shadows which were creeping up the valleys.

The Dallas Conundrum

Outside the 'Dallas' café rain was hissing down on Smithfield's pavements, muting the low diesel drone coming from the ranks of parked meat lorries. Their drivers sat at the small formica tables chatting, gulping tea and demolishing bright platefuls of fried food. It was nearly two o'clock in the morning.

Dick leant back in his chair to read the list of 'Dallas' specialities on the wall: beans, egg and chips; sausage, egg and chips; bacon, beans and chips; chips; black pudding . . .

'What's it to be then?'

'Horses are out.'

'OK, what about dogs?'

'They bite.'

'Mules?'

'Too slow.'

'A lot quicker than your 'Tricycles to the North Pole' idea.'

'At least it's different.'

'Look, I like the idea of doing something with animals . . .'

'Like eating them. Two black puddings and chips please. With tea.'

There was a truce while we ate. The problem was to think up a new adventure. Christmas was approaching fast, and Dick had ten days' clear holiday over the New Year. I too would be available at that time. It would have to be a quickie. It could be in the air, on foot, or on water, but bicycles were our forte. The world offered endless possibilities provided we could afford it; we were happy to consider any geographical zone. The only major consideration was that it should fit in with the Intermediate Technology motto 'Small is Beautiful'.

'What we need', said Dick with his best analytical frown, 'is something original, using low technology means, in a third-world country.'

'You mean like floating down the Amazon in an amphibious pram?'

Here the conversation went off at an inter-galactic tangent for quarter of an hour while we considered pogo-sticks, polar wastes, deserts, rollerskates, oceans, sailboards, rivers and rafts. By the time we came back to earth, it was time for more black pudding.

'How about Africa. Plenty of I.T. projects there.'

'Bike across the Sahara?'

'No good. Murph and Tim have already done that.'

'Swim up the Nile?'

'Don't like water.'

'Right. What about running somewhere. Cairo to Capetown? Up Kilimanjaro?'

'Did running last time.'

'Bike up Kilimanjaro then!'

'Mmmmm. Could be good. Could be BRILLIANT! Let's do it!'

'We need a name; something zappy. Kilimanjaro by Bike? Pedals to the Roof of the World? Soaring Saddles?'

And there it was; The Concept: riding bicycles up the highest mountain in Africa and one of the biggest volcanoes in the world to boot. Twenty Thousand Feet on Two Wheels had a ring about it. Intermediate Technology (I.T.) fitted in perfectly: Kilimanjaro squats solidly in the middle of East Africa, where I.T. has many projects. Dick's sister Bar and husband Rod lived in Nairobi and could help set things up at the African end. Bar furthermore had made an on-foot ascent of the mountain only the previous year. It was, as Dick said through a mouthful of cooked pig blood 'ace'.

(Dick) Bicycles have been in the Crane veins since our mothers pedalled pregnant to the ante-natal clinics. We'd been 'off-road' in our school days on sit-up-and-beg roadsters, but now we had the true 'mountainbike'. For the past 100 years, wheels and a triangular frame with pedals, brakes and a saddle have evolved to go faster and faster in a straight line on tarmac. Then, a couple of years back, the rough, tough cross-country bikes invented by Californians crossed the Atlantic. Interest spread like wildfire and mountainbikes took off across fell-sides, grassy tracks and through the forests. But no-one had tested a mountainbike on a real mountain, on snow and ice, at high altitude. Here was a golden opportunity for an exciting adventure. It had all the makings of a winner.

Speculation followed. Do good ideas always arise from agonised brain-storming sessions or are they really meant to occur in a flash of brilliant inspiration? Did Newton sit under an apple tree with fruit bouncing off his skull till sheer pain forced a conclusion? Or was a previously unopened catch in Newton's fertile mind sprung by the random connection of a Bramley with his cranium? These, and other important philosophical conundrums, would for the moment go unanswered because our seats were required by two very hungry looking drivers from Inverness.

Something in the City

We left the 'Dallas' and walked around the corner to Dick's bedsitter, a room-and-a-half over a taxi-driver's watering hole called 'The Tasty Cafe' in central London. At the time, I was temporarily living there while Dick spent his weekdays working in Aberdeen. It is a residence of some character and originality.

When you squeeze through the door, it looks on first sight to be utterly uninhabitable. It does on second sight too. The overall impression is of a cross between Everest base-camp and a rather run-down bicycle shop: in the centre of the

room is a Heath Robinson racking system constructed from wooden pallets supporting a couple of racing bicycles, a collection of wheels and cardboard boxes from the tops of which protrude an unnatural number of bicycle pumps. Rucksacks, sleeping bags and bundles of winter mountaineering clothing are stuffed in crevices. Beneath this lot is the desk on which stands a 1929 Imperial typewriter used for tapping out material for cycling and running magazines. Parking tickets and postcards from distant friends are piled below the crispy leaves of a long-dead spider plant. Books are kept in an old GEC fridge which has a heavy door that shuts with a satisfying 'clunk', and there's an upended ammunition box which serves as a seat for visitors (the resident's chair is a capacious chocolate-brown dralon recliner presented to Dick after crossing the finishing line of a quadrathon race).

A drying line (from which hangs a 'Bicycle Action' sweatshirt and a huge yellow inflatable banana) invites the eye to look left past a tandem frame and a crookedly-hung picture Dick brought back from Peru, towards the flat's nerve centre: the telephone. It sits on a school trunk and has a broken return spring in its dialler, so that calls can only be connected if the user can revolve the dial backwards at just the right speed. Behind the phone is another thirties tandem used as a shelf for phone books, ice axe, spare tyres and another dried-up pot plant. The whole room measures 12 feet by 18 feet.

Looking around the place, we both agreed it was the perfect operations centre for planning 'Bicycles up Kilimanjaro'. It was after all, an estate agent's dream: "a compact apartment in superb location, close to all services". Dick stuffed up a hole in the window to keep out the October draught and we unrolled our sleeping bags. I never needed an alarm clock in St John Street, because the fumes from the breakfasts being fried down below in 'The Tasty' poured through a vent into the room at 7.30 each morning. On days when bacon sandwiches were popular, the odour would be so potent you could virtually see the rinds reconstituting as the smell condensed on the flat's bright orange walls. I always woke in Dick's home feeling happy and optimistic; one just knew the day was going to get better.

(Dick's diary, 26 October 1985.) A lot of brainwork last night. Generated a good idea, but we might have been delirious. Forgot to turn off the leaky gas oven, but felt OK this morning. Big Kili by mountainbike still sounds ace. Culmination of years of cycling and climbing experience. And fun too. Must write to Ados [Dick's brother]. *He will be pleased. Also tell Nick that Ados and Karen named their son Jaro after the mountain because it means 'bright and shining' in Swahili. This is an Ados-type adventure. He's the archetypal lateral-thinker and he revels in dreaming up and attempting ludicrous projects. It was his inspiration which got 'Running the Himalayas' off the ground and laid the groundwork for this.*

We'll have to divide up the work-load in order to get everything organised in time. Nick can lay into bike firms. I'll use some smiles and waffle to get some mountain equipment. If necessary we do have most of the basics amid our accumulated junk and friends. We could do with some maps and background info on Kili, but most importantly we need to get the I.T. side of the fund-raising mobilised. Nick is raring to go.

'Big-K' needed to be up and running as soon as possible. We had 63 days before we'd have to be at the foot of a distant African mountain, complete with appropriate bicycles, equipment, food, a moderate amount of fitness, and enough knowledge to make sure we'd reach the top. Dick's holiday lasted from 22 December until 6 January. Knock off a couple of days for Christmas in Nairobi, another couple for re-assembling the bikes and checking the gear after the flight, and we were down to a span of eight days in which to make our ascent. There would be no time to spare, and it looked as if we'd just have the one opportunity to get it right; no latitude for bad weather or organisational foul-ups.

Going for IT

A visit to the Intermediate Technology offices in Covent Garden was one of the first items we'd biro'd onto a 'Dallas' paper napkin. For Dick there was an element of *déjà vu* in this; two years ago he and Ados had made a similar visit when, as tyro adventurers they'd arrived at the red door in King Street with a suggestion that they raise money for the charity by running the length of the Himalayas.

That proposal had met with incredulity, not only at I.T. but also from many other expedition experts. Dick and Ados persevered and went on to complete a continuous foot traverse along the mountains starting in Darjeeling and travelling through Nepal, Everest Base Camp, Kathmandu, into north-west India, Zanskar, the Tibetan plateau, Vale of Kashmir, and across Pakistan to Rawalpindi to finish. They covered more than 2,000 miles, climbing nearly 300,000 feet over 64 mountain passes in 101 days. They had no porters, no guides and carried no tent, no cooking equipment, no food, no water. They relied entirely on moving quickly and buying sustenance and shelter wherever possible. Over £60,000 was raised for I.T.

We went to see Steve Bonnist, the promotions officer for I.T. and the man who had master-minded the fund-raising that arose from 'Running the Himalayas'. For the months during and after the run, Steve had worked long into the night sifting diaries and photos as they dribbled back from 'the boys' (as he likes to call Dick and Ados) in Nepal and India, sending material to the press, drafting information releases, arranging lectures and generally making sure the charity was making the best of the opportunity.

(Dick) The charity tries to ensure that underprivileged people around the world receive the best benefit from the funds. All I.T. projects are long term, intended to stimulate jobs and community spirit in an area. Most are technologically or economically based in that the people receive something they can use to help work themselves out of poverty. Bicycle ambulances are built in Malawi, fishing boats in Sri Lanka, efficient cooking stoves in Nepal. Throughout each project the I.T. adviser works closely with local leaders to ensure preservation of local values and culture. These ideas were first widely promoted by Dr Fritz Schumacher in a book called Small is Beautiful. *It is from his inspiration that Intermediate Technology was formed in 1965. Steve Bonnist had been digging wells in Upper Volta when he joined I.T. in 1975. He's an ex-American who several times found himself being shot at in Ethopia. He maintains his tiny desk area in total disarray and is ridiculously excitable. Yet he is somehow able to cut through it all to identify the correct decisions and to isolate the phone calls and encouraging words that promote I.T. to its fullest.*

Steve reacted to 'Bicycles up Kilimanjaro' with customary enthusiasm:

'Oh no. You can't do this to me. You're mad, mad, MAD. D'you know you're mad? Jenny will divorce me. There'll be a tidal wave of letters and donations and I'll be working all hours. Oh no!'

A minute or two later: 'I love it. I love it. You're crazy!'

We explained that we required no help or money from Intermediate Technology. We would organise, finance and complete—or at least attempt—the expedition ourselves, and promote the fund-raising aims whenever and wherever possible. I.T. could print some sponsor leaflets, then use the funds we raised for their projects throughout the world.

Then Steve had a brainwave (distinct from the 'brainstorm' he'd just survived): why not raise money for a specific project? There was a desperate need for windmills to pump water in northern Kenya. The drought afflicting Ethopia was not just confined to that country, and there were desert regions in Kenya which could do with help. I.T. was involved because it had designed a windpump that was at present being built under licence near Nairobi. Each windmill cost £7,000 and provided long-term drought relief and also jobs in Nairobi. It seemed a realistic target for us to aim for. Steve said he'd put out feelers and find the most needy recipient for a Kijito windmill. Two weeks later he telephoned:

'There's a place up near the Ethiopian and Somali borders. A T.B. hospital. It's in the middle of a very hot desert, and they need running water. There is proven water underground but it is not possible at present to reach it. There are no phone links so we can't find out more at the moment, and it's a three-day journey from Nairobi . . . if things go well. Apparently there are bandits and you have to travel in armed convoys. The place is called Wajir. And you're not to go there!'

Big is Complicated

(Dick) We decided on a novel approach to organising the fund raising. We would put the word about that we were going to do something, somewhere, but the actual details would be obscure. This way we hoped to generate a little buzz among a wide group of people about our secret expedition. Then, when our fund raising effort was announced, we'd hopefully make a big splash. The I.T. drive would be more wide-ranging if concentrated into a few weeks initially.

We concocted a prospectus about our secret expedition, and called it 'The Next Quest'. It included a breakdown of costs. The reader would know only that we planned an expedition in snowy mountains in the southern hemisphere, and that mountainbikes were involved.

It was such a beautifully simple concept: two people on the most elegant form of human-powered transport, scaling one of the most romantic mountains in the world. Six weeks later, as we sat in the St John Street bedsit surrounded by overwhelming mounds of gear, and with four more people added to the team list, we wondered what had happened to our small and beautiful idea.

First class photos would be vital for pushing I.T. on our return. When Dick and Ados ran the Himalayas, they took all their own pictures, using the camera's action delay, and laboriously staging each frame. On Kilimanjaro, we just would not have time for that, and it would also be a lot harder to set up remote-controlled photos using bikes. We needed someone who was super-fit, and who could also take the pictures we needed. Pete Inglis lives in North Wales, on the island of Anglesey just across the Menai Straits from the peaks of Snowdonia; the view from his loo embraces most of the Carnedds, Glyders, Snowdon and Crib Goch and, if you lift yourself two inches, you get to see Garnedd-goch too. He's a teacher in a residential education centre, and his special interests include photography, local history, visiting exotic foreign locales and brewing beer. I phoned him late in the evening, hoping to catch him after his homebrew had lowered his resistance to crazy schemes:

'Great, when do we leave?' came the immediate response, then: 'Where did you say this hill is?' Pete and I had made several foreign trips together—cycling in France and Norway, skiing in Switzerland and Italy, white water rafting in Lapland—and we knew what made the other laugh, and what issues ended in white rage. Since Pete was going to accompany us right to the summit, all three of us had to be able to rely on each other completely; should an emergency arise, the trust had to be implicit.

We now found ourselves creating the logistical pyramid well known in Himalayan mountaineering, that has a large support team with the sole role of getting just one or two to the top. Dick and I might just have been able to survive for a week on the mountain entirely on our own, carrying all the food and equipment ourselves. But it wasn't physically possible for Pete to carry all his personal gear *and* food *and* 30lb of cumbersome camera gear *and* remain agile enough to scamper around taking photos of bouncing bikes. We were going to need a couple of porters to carry for us, and we were going to need someone to organise those porters. There was also the question of who would carry *The Sunday Times* photos and story down the mountain on New Year's Day. Dick and I were keen to stay on the summit for two, possibly three days in order to give plenty of time for some high-altitude cycling; it would be a great shame if we had to spend five days cycling up Kilimanjaro, then have to set off straight down again on a delivery errand.

We reckoned it would be handy to have three helpers—for organising porters, keeping an eye on the gear we weren't using, and getting the I.T. news material down the mountain. And although we didn't admit it at the time, both of us were intrigued to find out what it would be like to organise a 'proper expedition' where you had extra complications like logistics and personalities.

(Dick) Michèle Young was an obvious candidate. She's active, enthusiastic, full of alternative viewpoints and meticulously careless. A group of her language students were learning too slowly, so, off her own back, she organised a day trip to France, booked the ferry and meals, but turned up on the day without her passport! She makes friends easily and was sure to galvanise and direct the porters and guides. Michèle has experience and knowledge of local people because she worked for a year in the remote Kenyan village of Nzeluni half way to Garissa. She has also been subjected to two of the famous Scottish winter mountaineering expeditions organised by Hol [Nick's father], so she's no newcomer to wet, soggy clothes and being blasted by blizzards. I met Michèle some five years ago while conscripting members for the Reading University Pedalling Club. She was a bright-eyed fresher and we needed a social secretary. This motley band of bikers used to turn out most Sundays to cycle 10 or 20 miles, mend punctures, drink orange juice and halves of Guinness, and go home happy. When I was being pressurised by Ados to run the Himalayas, she sent me a postcard entitled 'L'Ultime Approche'. I was mad on bicycles; Ados was mad on mountains. It seemed logical to combine the two one day. The postcard showed a cyclist struggling up a snowy peak . . . feminine intuition. Now, two years hence, Michèle's postcard is particularly appropriate.

Catriona Hall, expedition artist and dare-devil parachutist, was the youngest in the team. An expert on Florentine and Sienese art in the 11th and 12th century, Kate hadn't been on a mountain before, so Kilimanjaro would be a moderately ambitious 'first'. She set about a rigorous training programme, testing her nerve by sticking her finger through the steel grilles of moving lifts, and improving her fitness by running across a corner of Clapham Common to the tube, on the way to work. Kate was also spotted sprinting up five flights of stairs while holding her breath 'so that I acclimatise to oxygen starvation'. She'd asked to be the one charged with getting *The*

Sunday Times material down to the bottom of the mountain.

With her experience of keeping hordes of horrid schoolboys under control, Maggie Birkhead would hopefully bring a touch of order to an otherwise off-beat group. Maggie had recently returned from an expedition to deepest Zimbabwe where she'd camped amid marauding lions and made a detailed study of rhinoceros droppings; she's a biology teacher, and knows much about the flora and fauna we'd be coming across in the jungle section of the ride. Maggie too hadn't been up a mountain, though she did claim to know what one looked like.

My cousin, or to give him his full title, Doctor Richard Charles Crane, was the fifth member of the team. Known as 'Dick', Dick (not to be confused with 'dik-dik' which is a small African antelope-type thing) is well-known for his ability to persevere beyond the bounds of comprehension in order to either succeed or to win. His skills at analysing problems would prove more than useful on the mountain while his memory—which is somewhere above the 16,384 kilobyte level—would save keeping notes. A remarkable ability to carry on thinking logically in the most desperate situations is a characteristic that had been useful in the past, and was certainly a confidence booster for others on Kilimanjaro. Dick had been training for Kilimanjaro by living in a tent out on the Scottish hills for two months, while working for BP in Aberdeen. He kept his suit in a filing cabinet and his running gear in a bottom drawer.

(Dick) Bringing up the rear of this motley band was the redoubtable Nick Crane. The first time I remember meeting him, he looked a real wimp with grey school trousers and round specs. He was getting out of a Land Rover to follow his father Hol, but his legs hardly reached the ground. Hol had come to Cumbria to lead us on one of his winter mountaineering expeditions to Scotland. Ever since we were old enough to walk, we had heard of this fabled annual ritual in which Hol and my father Charles had been involved since the end of their Oxford days. That particular year when I officially met Nick was our first invitation and we were fifteen. We did 10 days of walking and struggling around the remotest Scottish hills, and learnt a lot about snow, rain, cold and mist. After the first few days' training it turned out that I was reliable enough to proudly carry some of the chocolate for choccy halts.

Since those early days of goofy teeth and myopia, we've each been on at least ten of these confounded trips. We've learnt about survival and stamina, and most importantly we've learnt about people. Hol has whetted our appetites for more adventure, and Nick became so restless that after his degree at Cambridge he never settled down. I remember him with a Morris Minor van and a large but shaky motorbike and I guess he seriously wanted to be a normal person but couldn't afford it. Bicycles have opened the door to endless fun and opportunities. Nick has cycled in over 20 countries, and pedalled for 2 weeks amongst Corsican bandits with no more than a plastic sheet to hide under and a puncture repair outfit to defend himself. He got me involved in bikes and our principal claim to fame for many years was a 35-mile two-man team time trial at which we won a pair of socks.

Our expedition team was nearly complete when a letter landed on my doorstep at Expedition HQ. Hol had sent the signing-on papers for his own fiendish adventurer, a teddy bear which he sent us as our mascot. The pecking order was immediately re-structured. No longer was there only Nick and myself riding mountainbikes up Kilimanjaro. Now we were three: Kilimanjaro Teddy (KT), Nick and Dick. No, four: KT, N, D and Pete the photographer. Sorry, now we are seven: KT, N, D, P and Kate, Maggie and Michèle. Correction, wrong again, we are eight: KT, N, D, P, K, 2M and Steve Bonnist. How about our brothers and sisters and friends? And the equipment sponsors? Would Kilimanjaro itself like to be a member of its own expedition?

The Mountainbike Inheritance

Our planning time was suddenly cut down when I decided to go out to Kenya two weeks earlier than Dick. Pete was to come with me. With one week left before the advance party were due to fly, there was still an awesome number of tasks to complete. Dick was up in Aberdeen and I was camping in his bedsit, which was slowly filling up with crampons, balaclavas, cooking stoves, climbing ropes, sleeping bags, tents, candles, anoraks, snow shovels—but still no bikes. We knew what we wanted: mountainbikes. Over the years we'd both been periodically lured off the road, normally on unsuitable machinery and always with mixed success.

In common with most grazed-knee tear-assed schoolboys I invested much of my youth in riding bicycles where I shouldn't: building sites, woods, river banks, the sitting room and so on. There were accidents, and sometimes injuries. Those to the rider were normally repairable, but the bikes occasionally suffered more drastic damage. A green tricycle which had been appropriated from sister Liz to test its cornering ability on loose gravel, had a near-terminal collision with a brick wall. Later, a solid and rather fine 'fifties Sun tandem which steered like the *Titanic*, died after being ridden through a bush on the North Downs, which turned out to be hiding a Roman milestone.

Subsequently there were various expeditions onto the rough-stuff using a standard touring bike. Doug Whyte and I once tried to 'ride' to the southern-most tip of mainland Greece, Cape Matapan, following a thin skein of bouldery, thorn-strewn donkey tracks. We had to ditch the bikes and walk, after running out of puncture repair patches (family honour was however upheld, because two years later Hol managed to complete this trip, riding all the way, on a heavy-duty Raleigh roadster). There were other bold adventures using road bikes: together with Pete Inglis there was an incredibly rough crossing of the Picos de Europa mountains in northern Spain using 'pista para jeeps' with surfaces which would make a river-bed look smooth; again, punctures nearly landed us in trouble when I hit a rock at 8,000 feet during a wild storm with darkness fast approaching. The year before, again with Pete, stones and storms had got in the way of what would have been an interesting crossing of some wild mountains above Norway's Aurlandsfjord.

The limitations of road bikes were further underlined during several trips to countries whose normal roads are often rough gravel, interrupted by wash-outs. Portugal, Spain, Norway, Sweden, Greece and Africa were all crying out for return visits on a mountainbike.

The transition from riding *among* mountains, to actually cycling *on* and *up* them occurred one weekend in north Wales, while visiting Pete. I'd taken with me a

Bickerton 'portable', a small wheeled aluminium-framed folding bicycle, which is so light and compact that it can be strapped onto a backpack and carried quite easily. Much to the amusement of other hill-walkers on that sunny June day, I lugged the thing up to the top of a nearby mountain and then rode it down. It was a fantastically exciting sensation: creaming down the hard turf, jumping rocks and fording streams. In that one descent I learnt about lowering the saddle for greater control, and I also learnt that Bickertons are not ideally suited to 30 mph mountainside slaloms; the bike was never quite the same again.

Then in 1981, Geoff Apps, one of the first to build a true mountainbike in the U.K., lent me a prototype one weekend for an attempt to cycle up Snowdon, at 3,559 feet the highest mountain in England and Wales. The bike had tungsten steel studs in the tyres (which had been specially imported from Finland) and a bottom gear of 18 inches. Its performance was astonishing: the combination of gearing, traction from the tyres, and control from the frame geometry and wide handlebars made it possible to ride up wet, slippery, grassy and rocky slopes that would have been impossible on any normal bicycle. On only a couple of sections was I forced to get off and push, and then only because I was too physically exhausted to carry on pedalling; there seemed no limit to the obstacles this bike could tackle. I was hooked.

Three years later, when mountainbikes finally came on stream in the U.K., Marsh Norris (who crops up later in this story as the manufacturer of Marsh's Original Glacier Biscuits) and I borrowed a couple of the new 'Muddy Fox' machines and tried them out on the Ridgeway, the long rough track of mud and gunge that runs from the Thames down to the Marlborough Downs. We cruised the whole route easily in a day, and just couldn't find anything which could stop the bikes; I was disappointed. It seemed the moment to find a ride that would defeat the mountainbike, and thereby define its capabilities. The toughest mountain traverse I could think of which was within easy reach of the south-east of Britain was the 'Welsh 14 Peaks', a 22-mile rocky route over all the 3,000-foot mountains in Wales. And the most likely person I could think of who could break a mountainbike was cousin Richard.

Though we didn't know it at the time, the 14 Peaks was to be an inspiration for the Kilimanjaro jaunt, as well as being the learning ground for techniques and equipment we'd turn to later in the year as we prepared to set off for Africa. On the Snowdonia 'ride' we learnt that most mountainbikes are not supplied with low enough gearing. And we perfected the techniques of downhill control where, in order to keep both wheels on the ground, you have to lower the saddle and hang your backside right off the back of the seat. We found out just how tough mountainbikes are; neither of the Muddy Foxes gave a hint of trouble during the '14 Peaks'. And we discovered that for serious mountainbiking on rocky terrain, you need to wear footwear which has ankle protection: lightweight boots we thought, would be ideal.

But the most interesting discovery was one made by the ever experimental Dick, who, cursing under the uncomfortable weight of an unwieldy mountainbike as he tried to hump it up a 'V. Diff.' rock climb, realised that the best way to carry a mountainbike is not to rest it on one shoulder, as is the cyclo-cross practice, but to put your head right through the main frame triangle, and rest the bike's down-tube flat across both shoulders, partly supporting the weight by grasping the front of the

the frame in your hands. It was brilliant. Not only was it more comfortable, with a more even distribution of weight, but the bike was better balanced, enabling the carrier beneath to negotiate tricky scrambles quite safely. The bike could also be supported 'no hands' on really steep climbs.

For Kilimanjaro, we knew exactly what we were looking for in a mountainbike. Both of us had done a fair number of empirical tests on the bendability of normal bikes. Along with my sister's little green trike, and my Sun tandem, over the years I'd also shortened an old black roadster by riding into the back of a stationary Triumph Herald and modified the front end of a touring bike with the aid of a pothole. An early off-road bike I'd built up folded in two while failing to jump a log. Dick, who generally has to do things 'one better', had once time-trialled straight into a sports car and collected a head-full of stitches. On another memorable occasion during his bike racing career, he was presented with a £240 repair bill to a milk float following a navigational error on the A4. Not even Uri Geller could have produced objects so remarkably bent as those two racing bikes.

It was clear to us that ordinary bicycle tubing was not going to be enough to survive Kilimanjaro. These bikes had to be strong, and they also had to be mechanically slick enough to cope with fuddled brains at 19,000 feet. They had an added challenge in that precise mechanical adjustments are not one of Dick's greatest interests in life; a derailleur gear is only out of adjustment to Dick after it dives clean through the rear wheel and emerges the other side as a collection of shiny silver metal shavings. The combination of my clumsiness and Dick's disinterest in oily bits would mean that the expedition bikes would have to be virtually bomb-proof, fool-proof . . . Kili-proof.

Together with strength and slickness, the 'Kili-bikes' also had to be lightweight. Looking at a contour map lent us by a kind cashier in Stanfords International Map Centre, it became clear that there were sections of the route that were going to be impossible to ride. That would mean shouldering the machines for what might turn out to be long stretches. We certainly didn't want bikes that were overbuilt, because every pound of weight would make a very great difference slogging up a 45-degree slope at 15,000 feet.

Ten days before we were due to fly, I phoned Saracen Cycles in Coventry, and put to them a proposition. There was a long pause, as if the line had gone dead.

'You must be absolutely raving mad,' came the response, followed by a long sucking of breath. 'When do you want them by?'

'Friday.'

'We'll try, but it'll be difficult.'

K Minus 2

Dick's electronic alarm traumatised me into life, and I lay listening to the quick rustle as my cousin wormed his way out of his sleeping bag on the other side of the room, the clumps and curses as he collided with rucksacks and bikes on the way to the sink, the clang of kettle on porcelain and then (and it always made me wince) the atomic Whhoooomphh!! as the hot water geyser ignited with explosive violence. I sat up to see Dick reeling across the battlefield towards the stove as the dust drifted down.

(Dick's diary, 8 December 1984.) There is a latent energy bursting to get out. We've been pursuing the bicycle adventure for six weeks and we want action. Everything is very hectic as we gather together the paraphernalia of the expedition: food, equipment, support, finance. Despite this I feel a hiatus: we're back-pedalling waiting to be let loose on the mountain slopes. I personally dislike any physical preparations beyond picking up my coat and knapsack and leaving a note on the door: 'No milk for a long time'. Mental preparation is more my line. I enjoy perusing maps and planning routes and timings. I like to imagine myself out in the wild, hammering along.

For this expedition I feel that we have a good chance of success. Nick and I are capable, I believe, of getting the bikes up to 19,500 feet. It will be interesting to see how much is rideable; most of it I hope.

The problems on the expedition are more likely to stem from the support crew and the porters they are controlling. I've never done any expedition with a proper support crew and in fact have never had to organise more than a couple of people before. It will be a new experience, and quite fascinating in itself. Obviously if someone gets injured then we could be in for trouble. More worrying to me is that one of our friends might lose sight of the objective of the expedition and get bored or frustrated. We shall have to keep everyone closely involved with the activities to make them feel useful, but equally let them all be working on their own initiative and testing their own abilities.

The aim of this expedition is to finance the Wajir windpump by getting Nick and I plus two bicycles to the summit of Kilimanjaro. If we have to get there by New Year's Eve in order to maximise the fund-raising, so be it. We drop all other interests and go hell-for-leather for the target. There will be no time for, nor tolerance given to, sun-bathing, souvenir hunting or visiting museums. If anyone doesn't like the serious undertone of the expedition then they can leave when they will, but we're not altering our objective to fit them.

Only 48 hours were left before Pete and I were due to fly to Nairobi. We still had to take the bikes from their boxes and check them over, sort and pack all the equipment and buy enough food to last six people for eight days. Dick set off towards Holborn and the West End of London wearing an enormous rucksack, looking for head-torches, boots, compasses and extra-long tent pegs that could be used in ice. Kate telephoned, and found herself roped in to buying a large quantity of soup, milk powder and oats.

Then Pete walked through the door, just off the train from Anglesey. He was attached to a mammoth rucksack, and before he could even take it off, was on hands and knees fixing pedals to a mountainbike. *The Sunday Times* wanted to take some photos before we left. Dick and I were due at a photographic studio a mile away, in ten minutes' time, to arrange the shots that *The Sunday Times* were going to use to announce 'Bicycles up Kilimanjaro'. Five minutes later Kate stumbled up the stairs dragging festoons of plastic carrier bags stuffed with packets of food:

'Look,' she said, 'I hope I haven't made a terrible bish, but they only had Country Vegetable, so I got enough to make 7 gallons!'

'No Kate,' came a united chorus, 'we all *LOVE* Country Vegetable'.

Dick still hadn't returned, and we were already late for the photo session. The paper had asked to photograph all our equipment too, so Pete and Kate started hurling things into the biggest rucksacks they could find, then set off towards Gray's Inn Road bent under loads that would make the strongest Sherpa demand a pay rise. I leapt on the nearest mountainbike. The saddle shot down into the frame delivering a pile-driving blow to my coccyx, the handlebars swivelled round and the chain fell off. There was still a touch of fine-tuning to be done to the bikes before they'd be ready for Kilimanjaro.

We'd been at the studio ten minutes when Dick burst in, full of himself. He'd come across some 'ace headgear' for Kilimanjaro: a Helly Hansen thermal balaclava which he demonstrated could be turned into three different types of hat, depending on the weather and conditions. 'It's all in the folding you see. Look, here it's got a flap to stop your neck getting burned, fold it like this and it's got a sun visor; like this and it's good in a blizzard, open this flap and it lets the heat out . . .' It could even be worn as a balaclava. The credit for these discoveries goes to Ados Crane who, during the Himalayan run, had explored all the possibilities. Ados and Dick had used this balaclava as their sole headgear: suitable for snow and ice at Everest Base Camp and in the midday sunshine of the jungle. The hat was blue, and looked like a tea-cosy.

We stood for three hours in the bright white studio lights, then pedalled up to Primrose Hill so that Frank Herrmann, the photographer, could take some 'action shots'. There was a small hill that we had to ride up a lot of times; it wasn't particularly steep, and certainly didn't look impressive, but we just didn't seem able to make the bikes climb properly. For Dick it was a salutary lesson: 'We looked like real novices,' he complained when Frank had finished. 'If we're going to stand any chance on Big K we're going to have to improve quickly. Maybe there'll be somewhere in Kenya we can test the bikes before going to Kili.'

We left Primrose Hill knowing that the next time these bikes would be ridden in earnest would be on a different continent, under rather more severe conditions. The reality of the challenge was catching up on us. Suddenly it all looked a bit serious.

But on the way back to St John Street, as we were trying to out-accelerate each other away from the Camden High Street traffic lights, a familiar figure hailed us from the curb. It was Richard Ballantine, bicycle guru; author of the book which made mending bicycles more à la mode than muesli; radical inspirer of the more weird and wonderful aspects of cycling and devoted mountainbike aficionado. Casting an appreciative eye over our new machines, he pointed at the lightweight ice-axe strapped to one of the bikes and allowed us the ultimate accolade: 'Wow. That's a nice image.'

It felt like the final blessing.

Back at the bedsit, Pete was sitting with his feet on a stack of sleeping mats and tents, big red mug of steaming tea at his elbow, digging detritus from the bowl of his pipe while loud guitary rock music hammered off the walls. How was it he always looked so relaxed while all around him were in barely controlled frenzy? Dick was by now 'really revving' and wanted to go to a party in Reading that evening. This would be our last chance to say goodbye to Klon, Nigel, Elaine and assorted friends.

It was 4 am before I turned in. Three hours later I was up again, typing The Sunday Times report. Dick returned by lunch time, stayed for some photos in the afternoon, then headed north in the late evening.

(Dick's diary, 9 December 1984.) We did a photo session for Intermediate Technology in the afternoon. This evening, in mid December, marks a turning point in the expedition. Nick flies out to Nairobi tomorrow. Nearly all the gear has been packed and is ready to fly. All he has to do is get it, and the three bikes out to Heathrow and persuade the airline to give us excess luggage free to Kenya. I left Nick an hour or so ago, plodded across London to King's Cross with my clothes wrapped in a blanket and caught the London to Aberdeen Nightrider. Nick was sitting shell-shocked amid a mêlée of boots, crampons, paperwork, rucksacks and expedition gear. His hair was tufted, eyes bloodshot and staring. Poor old chap. 48 hours of whirlwind activity and he's wasted. How he managed to cycle across Europe in three weeks living on semolina, I'll never know.

It was 7.15 the next morning before I collapsed into a sleeping bag for a few minutes kip. For the hour or so it took to make the journey out of London to Heathrow I relaxed, beginning to think that the worst of it was now over. We walked into Terminal One feeling as if nothing could now stop 'Bicycles up Kilimanjaro'.

'And what's in those boxes then?' said the man at the check-in desk when confronted by a pile of accompanied luggage that Pete could scarcely see over.

'Bicycles,' I replied somewhat meekly, half expecting that such a harmless form of transport would elicit immediate sympathy and a complete waiving of what promised to be an astronomical excess baggage charge. The man was unmoved.

'Put it all on the scales.' We did so, and the needle did several revolutions before halting at a weight approximately equivalent to £1,300 worth of excess charges. Pete sank slowly out of sight behind the luggage mountain. I asked to see the manager. Presently he appeared, and we had a very fruitful discussion, during the course of which the future of 'Bicycles up Kilimanjaro' changed from one of potential bankruptcy, to one of being slightly skint for a while.

Five hours later, at Nairobi airport, we were faced with a not unfamiliar predicament: 'We must charge a percentage of these bicycles' value, as import duty. Let me see. They are worth £400 each, that makes it, um 5,000 Kenyan shillings. You can pay over there.' Pete gulped and started sinking again: 5,000 Kenyan shillings was a lot! The customs officer who had made the invitation to relieve us of so much money looked especially unmalleable. 'Look' I said, 'we're just bringing them into the country for three weeks, then we'll take them away again. We don't want to sell them here'.

'Yes, I understand. The charge is 5,000 shillings. Pay, or if you like you can leave them at the airport and collect them on your return.' The options were not attractive: the chances of our finding the money were not high and the idea of dumping the bikes at Nairobi for the duration rather defeated the point of the expedition. Unless . . . what we could do is leave them the mountainbikes, and hire a couple of African bikes. OK they wouldn't be much good on the really treacherous sections of the mountain but we could probably ride them occasionally, particularly down in the jungle sections. And if they fell apart, which they almost certainly would, then we'd just carry the bits the whole way to the top. Somehow, we were going to get bicycles up Kilimanjaro.

I put the 'African bike option' to Pete. He rolled his eyes and told me to calm down.

'Something'll happen,' he said. By now we were the only people left in the Arrivals Lounge. Us and our seven rucksacks and three big brown boxes. The man in the white gold-braided uniform was chatting with customs officers and occasionally glancing our way. Another idea: 'Pete, we could wait till he gets bored with us, then just rush out past customs when nobody's looking.'

'Nick, first, how do you rush anywhere with 130 kilogrammes of luggage; second, where are you proposing we rush to—this airport appears to be in the middle of precisely nowhere and third, don't you think that, if you do start rushing anywhere, one of these men with the big sticks and peaked hats is going to walk over and whack you more than gently? Anyway . . . did you know that someone's waving at you from the other side of the barrier?'

I looked up. It was Bar, Dick's elder sister, resident of Nairobi and old hand at understanding bureaucracy. It took her just two hours to snip away the red tape and get our boxes and bags out into the grey drizzle of Kenya. The Land Rover springs creaked as yet another colourful rucksack was jammed in the back, and Bar asked what our plans were for the fortnight until Dick was due to arrive.

'Well,' I said, 'we'd like to visit a place called Wajir.'

Number Nine North

Back at Bar's house, we spread the maps out on the verandah. On my atlas back in London, Wajir is shown as an isolated black dot on the edge of the Boji Plain in the north-eastern tip of Kenya. Just over a hundred miles to the north are the dusty plains and peaks of Ethiopia; fifty miles east is Somalia. On Bar's slightly more detailed map, Wajir has a spider's web of thread-like lines radiating out into the surrounding desert. Two of the thicker lines pointed in the direction of Nairobi.

All we had to do was find a means of moving along one of these lines. At the Catholic cathedral in Nairobi, they had heard of a couple of Sisters who worked in Wajir, but they'd left town the previous day, travelling so they thought, by truck. The journey apparently took three days. We telephoned the Kenyan Police, and they told us we could only reach Wajir by armed convoy: 'It's very dangerous for foreigners; there are many *shifta* (bandits)' they told me. At AMREF, the Flying Doctor Service, they were no more optimistic: 'We fly there occasionally; there's a small air-strip, but nobody makes the journey by road.'

The next hope was the Nairobi-based journalist for *The Sunday Times,* Mary-Anne Fitzgerald. She hadn't heard of anyone visiting Wajir before, neither had Mohamed Amin, the cameraman who'd broken the news of the Ethiopian famine a few months earlier. I was getting a touch desperate by now; time was ticking away, we'd already been in Nairobi for three days, and didn't seem to be getting anywhere. Everybody we spoke to about Wajir seemed either never to have heard of the place, or appeared to be pessimistic about the chances of reaching it. Finding someone who knew someone else who'd been to Wajir was difficult; finding somebody who had actually been there themselves seemed as likely as meeting an actuary who'd played bowls on the Great Barrier Reef.

On the fourth day, Bar (once again) solved the problem. I'd just put the phone down, having been told by a government agency that to use the road to Wajir one had to travel with police permits, which were only available on consideration of written application, at Police Headquarters in Nairobi. I related this information to Bar, who was sitting nearby.

'Permits! Why on earth should you need a permit to travel in Kenya—it's a free country.' She dived for the phone, and made a string of calls to missionary societies, doctors, pilots; in fact anyone she could think of who might have actually pulled off the impossible and reached the unreachable: Wajir. It didn't take her long to come up with the information we'd been looking for all week. It came from a Mr Warner.

'Take a bus from Nairobi to Isiolo, then either wait for another bus—there's one every three days—or catch a truck across the desert to a little place called Habaswein, where you must join a convoy for the last stretch to Wajir'. It seemed so simple. The time factor was a bit risky: if it took three days to reach Wajir and another three to return, we'd only just get back to Nairobi in time for Dick's arrival, and our departure for Tanzania.

Bar sensed this, and being the motivator that she is, told us at 4.30 that afternoon to 'Get going!'. We decided to travel light. We packed a jersey and hat each, a camera, a couple of water-bottles and some film. And a toothbrush. We wouldn't take sleeping bags, and at night we'd sleep under the stars if need be. Hopefully we'd be able to buy chapaties to eat along the way. I was really looking forward to the prospect of leaving all the hassles and bureaucracy behind for a few days, and travelling with a minimum of gear and a good friend.

Bar dropped us off at the OTC bus station near the mosque in downtown Nairobi. There was a bus due to leave at 9 pm, but all the seats had been sold. A man wearing a green corduroy jacket, who appeared to be the bus station manager, gave us an address in a distant Nairobi suburb where, he said, we might be able to pick up a couple of unclaimed tickets. Off we rushed, running for a beaten-up bus loaded to the roof with Africans returning home from work. The address we'd been given didn't exist, but we did find a youth in a kiosk selling cigarettes, who claimed to be the OTC agent we were looking for. No, he didn't have any tickets, but would we like any cigarettes? Or sweets?

With panic setting in and darkness approaching, we decided to get back to the OTC bus station. We leapt on a passing *matatu*—a small 12-seater bus with a technicolour interior plastered in garish painted designs, tassles and coloured lights, and a young African lolling coolly at the open door with a Camel at his lips and an enormous radio blaring beat music at his feet. The audio-visual effect of this bus ride could only be simulated by staging a disco in a biscuit tin. We made it back to the bus station in time to catch 'Green Cord', relating to him our unsuccessful odyssey into the dangerous back-waters of Nairobi.

'Wait here,' he said. Two minutes later he walked briskly through the yellow door of his office, arm outstretched, broad smile on his face, and handed us two tickets on the Number Nine to Isiolo:

'I have made an arrangement, so there are two spare tickets. Take these. You will find the night bus is very fast. No problem. Quick bus to Isiolo.'

We found a place each to sit on the bus. The seats were of the bench variety, and were wide enough to seat two people side by side. We sat three to a seat, with another fourteen people standing in the aisle. The night was hot, and we sat with a sheen of sweat on our faces and forearms, waiting for the bus to move, longing for a draught to cool us down. Just before leaving, 'Green Cord' appeared, wriggling past the passengers in the aisle. 'God be with you gentlemen' he said, and shook each of us by the hand.

'Bicycles up Kilimanjaro' was developing a knack of attracting saintly souls at just the right moments.

A Ride on the Wild Side

The night, fortunately, went quickly. Sleep was impossible, as the bus swayed and bounced over the pitted tarmac. Both Pete and I were sitting on the aisle end of a seat, with just one buttock hooked onto the thin padding. Relax, and you would fall to the floor. Thika and Muranga slipped by the windows, and the bus began a long climb north towards Mount Kenya. At Nyeri everyone dashed for the door, and peed into the blackness beside the bus, then turned, hobbled across the road with stiff legs and drank hot sweet tea in the 'Snow View Cafeteria'. In the early hours the bus flashed past a big sign depicting a black-painted Africa with a red line across its centre; we'd crossed the equator.

Isiolo is the last big town on the road north; there's not much beyond this dusty outpost other than scrub and desert. Our bus pulled into the main street half an hour before dawn, and, thankful for the sudden stillness and quiet, every passenger keeled over onto a neighbour's shoulder and went straight to sleep. An hour later, the sun peeked over the low hills of Mukogodo just outside the town, and quickly filled the bus with new light and heat. To call our arrival point the 'main street' is a slight understatement. Isiolo is split down the middle by a dusty way at least a hundred yards wide, planted arbitrarily with small trees, and lined on both sides by a row of single-storey shops with coloured facades. Those along the western side of the street sang with red, yellow and brown materials, sparkling tin buckets and pans, and the gentle shifting of early-morning shoppers. Some of our fellow travellers had alighted and slipped into the *chai* (tea) house by which we were parked, and were now sitting silently, sipping the sweet tea and munching maize cakes.

Pete set off to enquire about the next bus to Wajir, and to buy food for the next couple of days. When he returned, he looked pleased: 'You won't believe this, Nick, but there's a bus leaving for Wajir in an hour. Or so they say! I've even bought some grub.' He had a sheet of newspaper wrapped around a couple of packets of biscuits and a plastic bag of maize cakes. Again we'd struck lucky: there was only one bus to Wajir every three days, and we'd just happened to arrive on the right morning. We bought tickets, and occupied two of the last remaining seats on the bus. They were not exactly in a prime position. It was the same bench arrangement as before, but this time we had space for two up against a window, right above the rear wheels. The seat had been bolted to the floor crookedly, reducing what modest leg-space there was to a narrow slot that was barely wide enough to take a single foot, let alone a pair of long legs and size 10 feet. It was going to be a long journey.

We took turns to walk about outside till the bus was ready to leave. Two men were flat on their backs under the engine, probing an oily orifice with a length of wire, and up top under a climbing sun, another was catching hessian bags of merchandise that were being slung up from below. Long ropes trailed down from the roof to the dust, like loose rigging lines on a ship. When the packing was done, canvas tarpaulins were dragged over the whole, and the ropes were used to truss up the baggage tight to the roof rack. I talked in the shade of a tree to a man called Harrison, who worked as a water engineer in Mandera, on the Ethiopian border. He said that last time he'd made this journey, he'd been in a truck which had broken down in the desert. They'd had to drink the radiator water, and light a fire at night to keep the packs of hyenas at bay.

27

He said hyenas were so strong they could tear off a human arm.

The bus eventually lumbered out of Isiolo, lurching from side to side on the ridges and canyons of the dirt road, with fifteen people standing in the aisle. You had to clench every muscle in your body to prevent serious injury. The driver was no slouch, and on anything except raw untravelled desert (onto which we had to turn when the road disappeared) he would wind the old Leyland up to terminal velocity and keep his foot firmly on the floorboards. Dust poured in through the windows, and with every bump you'd have to brace yourself against the seat in front. Every couple of hours Pete and I swapped seats. The slot by the window had the advantage that you could, at the time when dust wasn't pouring in, stick your head out into the breeze and escape from the infernal bedlam of the bus interior; the price for this luxury was a sitting position that anaesthetised everything from the waist down.

Release from this purgatory came at a desolate spot called Kula Mawe ('eat stones'), when one of the bus tyres punctured. Pete acquired a couple of cold chapaties and a bowl of goat stew, and I sat on a wooden walkway watching the wheel being changed. I wondered how Dick was getting on back home, and whether he'd managed to buy all the last-minute items I'd been unable to bring out to Kenya with me. I'd phoned him from Nairobi, reading out a long list of things like torch bulbs, glucose tablets, solid-fuel, lubricating oil, a spare jacket and so on.

(Dick's diary, Friday 14 December 1984.) Nick telephoned today. Lucky lad is on a real adventure. Not much happening here in G.B. Christmas decorations are up in the main street of Aberdeen, carols blast out of shop doors and pubs. It's pouring with rain. The wettest November in 80 years and I'm still camping out. The building-site I've been using has been flooded out so I've moved the tent to wasteground nearby. This Wild Country hoop-tent from Blacks is fantastic. Several companies have offered to help with last-minute gear. No-one at B.P. knows I'm going on an exotic holiday this Xmas. Work as per usual: microscopes, maps, rock analyses and drilling rigs. No doubt Nick and Pete are enjoying themselves.

The rains had just finished, and in places the dirt road was flooded and the bus would have to slow down and swim through the brown water with a broad bow wave fanning out and washing on the small pale shrubs at the road edge. We passed a water-tanker, abandoned and listing, water resting on the lower sill of the open driver's door. It was always touch and go whether we'd make it through these long muddy lakes; the bus wheels would slither and spin sending up arcs of sparkling spray and every head would crane from a window to watch the action.

By mid-afternoon, the mountains behind us had disappeared into the heat haze, and the vegetation, which earlier had been full and lush, was now little more than stunted scrub. At Garba Tula we bumped over a low wooden bridge spanning a dry creek and parked outside the police post while the driver's documents were checked. Children rushed from the huts and tried to sell maize and bundles of *miraa*, a small plant which we are told is a stimulant when chewed; there was a man sitting three seats away who had been eating it continuously since the bus left Isiolo, and from his expression you'd think he'd drifted off to another solar system. But before any *miraa* purchases could be made, the driver was back in the seat. The whisper along the bus was that we were now so far behind schedule that we wouldn't be able to reach Wajir that night. The travelling merchant sitting in front of us became quite angry.

The road got worse, and in places we'd be down to walking pace as the driver had to steer the bus off into the desert, threading his way gingerly between thorn trees to bypass huge mud-pans and lakes. Mado Gashi is a very isolated spot. It sits at the junction of two tracks, has three *chai* houses and little else. Soldiers stopped the bus at a checkpoint on the far side of the village. Everyone went very quiet, straining to hear what they were saying to the driver. Voices were raised; people on the bus muttered. What were they saying? That the bus could go no further? *Shifta?* Too late to go into the desert? A few got off the bus and joined the driver and soldiers. Nobody seemed to know what was happening. We sat and waited, and it became dark.

Harrison, our engineer friend, presently came with news: 'Not good,' he said. 'The soldiers will not permit us to proceed. They say it is dangerous to travel to Wajir in the dark. We have to wait until tomorrow.' We went off to a *chai* house with Harrison and another, a thin man wearing a cloak, who bought us each a Fanta orange. When it was late, Pete and I climbed the ladder onto the roof of the bus, found a trough in the baggage, and lay listening to Mado Gashi preparing for the night. It was very dark, with no moon. Below us on the dust beside the bus squatted two circles of travellers. A couple of paraffin lamps cast pools of light on the rugs before them. One group had a transistor radio which was playing eastern dance music. There was a low wash of quiet conversation, like gentle waves on a soft shoreline, and we tugged the tarpaulin up to our shoulders to keep off the dew. The stars were bright as diamonds on black velvet, and I went to sleep blissfully content.

We were woken by the engine starting. It was six o'clock. Harrison told us that the driver was hoping to reach Wajir by the afternoon. An hour up the track, and we were into a proper desert, the Hothori, flat as a featureless for as far as the eye could see, with nothing growing higher than a few inches. In the middle of this featureless expanse, the bus stopped at a collection of huts: Habaswein. Here we had to take on our escort of three soldiers. The final 70 miles to Wajir, through the heat of the day, were memorable. I made a few notes in my diary:

> The inside of the bus is a continual din of rattling windows, each one clattering loosely in its frame like an orchestra of crazed castanets. There are 80 people on board, 20 of them trying to stand in the aisle, hanging on to seats and the metal stanchions of the roughly welded roof. Our armed escort is up near the door, rifles in their hands. We passed two army lorries draped in dozy soldiery. One has a bonnet up with two men fiddling inside. A youth stands on one of the cab roofs with two belts of machine-gun bullets across his chest.

Wajir

We spent that night in a bare, square room, empty except for a single bed draped with a tent of mosquito netting. It was hot enough to lie naked and still sweat till dawn. Wajir is virtually cut off from the outside world: no phones, no electricity (apart from a couple of generators), and surrounded by desert. There's a small airstrip used by the aid organisations and military. Wajir has had more than its fair share of hardship.

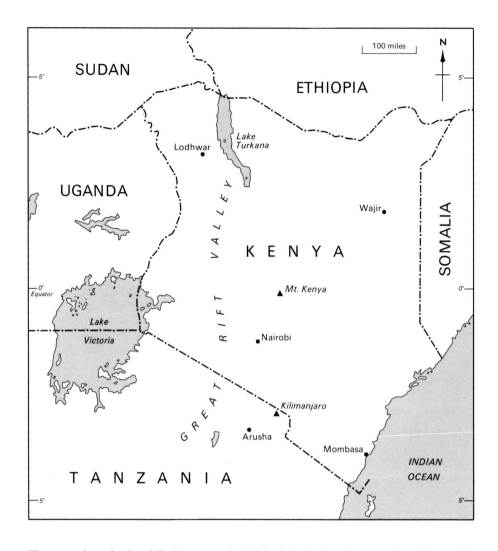

The same drought that killed so many in Ethiopia had wiped out nearly all the cattle in the region. The people are nomads, relying on cattle, camels and goats for sustenance. Many of the wells had dried up, and various aid teams had been active in the area for months. Bedford trucks full of grain and beans had driven up from Mombasa on the coast, and distribution points had been set up in the country surrounding Wajir. At the time we were there, a measles epidemic was rampant, and hundreds of children had already died. Then an official from the International Red Cross told us of a massacre just north of the town the year before. He said that scores of men from one of the local tribes had been herded into a fenced airstrip and left to starve in the sun. Reports vary; some say 1,400 were killed, others say it was closer to 3,500. The IRC man said there were something like a thousand families with no man.

On the first morning, Pete and I walked along a white dusty road to the TB 'Manyatta' hospital. It was strange to be suddenly confronted with what in London had been a single abstract phrase. Our 'TB hospital' turned out to be 250 small brushwood shelters loosely grouped around a concrete building which housed the visiting doctor's equipment. In the shade of the shelters and scrubby trees, patients sat singly and in knots, chewing *miraa,* chatting, watching; the air wracked every few minutes by the coughing and spitting of infected lungs. A young boy invited us inside one of the shelters. It was a low stoop through the small entrance and inside there was just room for two beds made from a trellis of sticks bound together with string. We sat on one of the beds till our eyes adjusted to the absence of sunlight. There was nothing in there but the beds. The sun filtered through small cracks in the thatch, casting tiny spots of light on the sandy floor. It was dark and cool. The boy whose home it was looked about fourteen, and spoke quite good English. He'd been living in the Manyatta for many weeks. Most of the patients stayed for six months; one man told us he'd been there for two years. Chemotherapy is being used here with much success. Once recovered, the patients return to their families and herds.

Tuberculosis is a debilitating disease; many of the Manyatta's patients were desperately thin. Despite this they had to make regular journeys from their huts to the nearest water source, a single tap on the far side of the road. This tap serves the entire hospital, and the medical staff too. All the water for drinking and washing had to be laboriously carried in a multitude of chipped enamel bowls and buckets, mugs and pans. The doctors have to fetch water from the tap for their medical analyses.

It didn't need much imagination to see the need for a water source on the site of the hospital. Already a storage tank was being built next to a disused well, right in the centre of the site. But there was no means of raising the water. Steven Wales, an aid worker, told us: 'The patients here are not strong enough to raise the water themselves, which rules out buckets; and hand-pumps are unreliable. So a windmill to pump the water up to the storage tank would be "appropriate technology" for the TB Manyatta.'

There was beauty and suffering in Wajir. The town was on the frontier of existence. Culturally the settlement seemed irrelevant to the people of the region; the wandering Somali nomads traditionally had no use for a town. They were self-contained, travelling with their camels, goats and cattle through the bush, with their brushwood shelters lashed to the camels. Wajir had acted as an unintentional focus: the place where the International Red Cross dispensed the famine relief; where Oxfam handed out goats to families who had lost them in the drought; where widows could be paid Kenyan shillings for irrigating *shambas.* And where TB, the disease no-one liked to talk about, could be cured. Life in Wajir was pared down to the minimum; survival was all that mattered. Faced with the scale of the need, providing one windmill seemed a pathetically inadequate gesture. It was nothing to write home about.

On the third night in Wajir we ate with Steve. He had one meal a day, in the evening, and, as it had been every evening for the past six months, he ate goat meat, cabbage and boiled potatoes. Afterwards I went to our stone 'cube' (as Steve called his home) to write my diary:

'I'm writing this by the light of a paraffin lantern perched on the edge of our communal bed. Pete is chasing a huge bug across the floor. Up in the dim ionosphere of the room (the tin roof is 15 feet above our heads) others bugs periodically collide with the walls and fall to the floor with a clatter. Mosquitoes are biting us continually. Pete earlier lit two mosquito coils; spirals of green stuff that smoke gently all night. Steve says they make your eyes go red. He's had malaria several times already. Outside the sky is a dense sprinkling of sparkling stars. There's a cicada in the room somewhere that's setting up a ceaseless staccato of chirruping; enough to drive you mad.'

We left Wajir the next morning. It wasn't an honest departure. I could feel the watching eyes of those who had to stay; those for whom there was no escape-route back to that other, comfy world of health, wealth and ignorance. Accepting the luxury of leaving Wajir meant we'd committed ourselves to these people no more than a television viewer would do to a drought-documentary. We were switching off the episode so that we could move on to the next activity. I saw the mildly uncomfortable journey out and back from Wajir as a token penance for this superficial commitment. White people normally flew.

A bus was rumoured to be due in Wajir that morning. Not unexpectedly, it didn't turn up. We were sitting drinking sweet tea in the shade, wondering when the next lorry would leave Wajir, when Mohamed (every male seems to be a Mohamed), a smiling youth who cleaned the tables and floors in three of the *chai* houses, rushed over to us and said 'Come quick, I've found you a truck.' We followed him into the light and heat.

It was a green Toyota pick-up, heading west across the desert. We managed to squeeze in the back, along with eleven others. The driver, a racy young man in a red shirt, had made an arrangement with the police, and we were to travel without an escort. He drove fast, leaving town trailing a plume of dust. The back of the pick-up measured about 8 feet by 5 and was covered by a heavy canvas tarpaulin, with two openings at the back just big enough to crawl through. The eleven of us were jammed inside, braced against the wild jolting and bouncing, bodies bashing non-stop on the metal floor and sides of the truck. In the semi-darkness I could see the other faces, expressionless and glistening with sweat. There was a strong smell of bodies.

At the first *chai* house, we stopped for an hour because our driver lent his spare wheel to another truck. We sat on the sand chatting with a smiling man called Jackson, who was travelling home for Christmas, a journey which he said would take him three days. He told us of a nomad he'd met in Mandera who was sick and asking for 200 shillings to pay for the bus fare to Isiolo, where there was a hospital. Nobody would give the man 200 shillings. And then it turned out that he owned 300 camels and 1,000 sheep, the equivalent of a small fortune. When Jackson asked him why he didn't sell a couple of the beasts to finance his bus ride to hospital, the nomad replied that he couldn't sell his animals, because they were his family's livelihood. Without them they would starve. But he couldn't afford the money for the hospital without selling; an impossible dilemma. And, he said, even if he did sell, he would be cheated. Jackson shook his head.

'They are different, the nomads. Animals are their life. They would rather die themselves than lose them.'

Halfway across the desert the truck became bogged down in the middle of the

Above: Probably the first time bicycles were ridden on the ridge of Crib Goch was 30 June 1984 during our traverse of the Snowdonia 14-Peaks; a cycle-ride with a difference which whetted our appetite for a taller challenge.

Below: Wajir, in arid north-east Kenya, where there are serious water problems; life for the people by this brushwood shelter would be made more tolerable by the erection of a windpump which could raise water from deep underground for drinking, washing, animals and growing crops.

flattest, hottest expanse of Africa imaginable. We all piled out into the searing heat and light, and watched while the driver spun the wheels and the truck sank to its floor in a sticky grey quagmire. We were in the middle of the *shifta* area and nobody seemed too keen to hang around. One of the older men in our little group who had yet to speak to anyone, grabbed the shovel from the back of the truck and plunged it into the mire. The handle snapped off with a loud crack and he threw it aside, going down on all fours and attacking the mud manually with the ferocity of a rampant Jack Russell on the scent of a bone; mud was flying in all directions. Everyone joined in, scooping and squelching, trying to clear a path for the jeep's wheels. It took half an hour of digging and shoving to release the vehicle. Once free, everyone dived in through the rear openings, and 'red shirt' gunned off towards Garba Tula. Here, our friend Jackson got in a spot of bother with the police, who had ordered us all out and searched the vehicle. In Jackson's bag was a new thermos flask, which had come across the Somali border. He had no receipt. After a lot of shouting by the police, and a marvellously authentic display of incomprehension by Jackson, he was allowed to keep the thermos, and we carried on westwards.

We'd been in the back of the truck for nine hours, when Pete shouted that he could see mountains ahead. The desert was coming to an end. The truck left the main track, striking off to the left along a very narrow trail which began to climb towards the forest of Meru. Bushes began to scrape the side of the truck, and now there were big trees. I managed to stick my head out of the side for a moment, and caught a thorn branch in my hair. I tried again and had an elevating glimpse of yellow butterflies flickering over muddy puddles. We changed down a gear and began a climb which lasted an hour. Behind us, the desert was dropping away, a frightening frying pan of heat-haze. It felt good to be away from it. Half-way up, the driver stopped and poured a bucket of water over the engine to cool it down; the whirling fan caught the water and flicked it out into the sunshine, a prickly spray on hot smiling faces.

Dusk was approaching by the time we reached tarmac. We'd re-crossed the desert in less than half the time it had taken by bus on the outward journey. As we stood with Jackson, waiting for a *matatu* to take us to nearby Meru, I had an idea:

'Pete, we've got a spare day now. How about going for a walk on Mount Kenya before heading for Nairobi?'

'Sounds OK,' but Pete at the time was more interested in massaging back to life a body which had been numbed by ten hours of torment in a steel torture chamber.

In Meru we said goodbye to Jackson, who told us he was stopping for the night because he was too tired to continue. He helped us find another *matatu* before walking off to find an hotel. Our *matatu* cruised round the town looking for a few more passengers then set off over the flanks of Mount Kenya to Nanyuki. We had very little money left between the two of us, and it took some time before we found the cheapest hotel in town.

A couple of hours later, replete with mixed grill and a mash of maize, potato and cabbage, we were planning our quick foray onto Mount Kenya. I went upstairs to try to phone Bar, to let her know we would be back in a couple of days. The pips were going when a knee was thrust into my groin, and I was pinned against the wall by an enormous lady.

'Where you goin' tonight then?' she demanded.

'Nnn...nn...nowhere. I'm staying here actually.'

'I'll be downstairs,' and she went down the steps with the subtlety of a filing cabinet falling down a lift-shaft. Slow on the uptake as ever, I returned to Pete a few minutes later, to find him fighting a rearguard action against my acquaintance of a few minutes ago, and another even larger lady who called herself Grace. There was a look of panic in his face:

'Nick, you know what this is don't you?'

'One star hotel?'

'It's a brothel!'

Left: Early excitement and firm trails in the lower jungle.
Above: Various experiments with methods of carrying bicycles convinced us that spreading the weight across our shoulders was the least painful option.
Below: Kilimanjaro National Park provides overnight facilities for trekkers at Mandara Hut; we camped on the edge of the clearing.

Come Together

(Dick) I said to the others a few weeks ago that since they are new to the joys of high climbing, altitude sickness may be an interesting experience. The first and foremost rule is to ascend slowly and rest frequently. To quote our expedition doctor, Mike Townend of Cockermouth who is himself an experienced Himalayan climber: 'No problems are likely to occur below 10-12,000 feet almost irrespective of how quickly or strenuously you reach that height. From then on, your chances of running into difficulties will be increased by cold conditions, hypothermia, dehydration, strenuous exertion or exhaustion, and of course the more rapidly you ascend the more difficult it becomes to acclimatise adequately. If you are trying to cycle to the top in the shortest time possible then you will probably just have to take pot luck, otherwise it would be wise after at least one night at 10-12,000 feet to acclimatise for a day or two at 15,000 feet before making a dash for the summit.'

I have had the misfortune of experiencing altitude sickness before, due to over-enthusiastic escapades on Mount Kenya with Ados in schooldays, Cotopaxi in Ecuador and the Rohtang La in Nepal. The thin air causes intense breathlessness, headaches, nausea and fatigue.

Mike Townend had supplied us with a new drug called Diamox, which helps one's body acclimatise. The effect is to keep one's acclimatisation always one day ahead of one's height in the mountain. We were scheduled to start the Diamox two days before we reached 10,000 feet, i.e. on Boxing Day. I knew that Nick and Pete were going to get high on Mount Kenya if they had the time, and I really hoped they would take the opportunity for some serious acclimatisation.

'Of course it'll be such useful experience,' I said over breakfast in the brothel.

'We'll be able to get up to about 14,000 feet where the air's good and thin, and we can get used to altitude headaches.' Pete looked pensive; he hadn't been over 9,000 feet yet, and was naturally wondering how he'd cope higher up.

'We've got to get to the bloody thing first.' We walked out into the white light of Nanyuki main street, spotted a British army lorry and followed its three tenants into a tea shop. They were on the way to Nairobi with thousands of empty beer bottles and plans to made amends for several weeks of celibacy. We travelled in the back with one of the soldiers, hanging on to the roof as the truck bounced along the lumpy tarmac at 60 mph: 'You f...... wanna be f...... careful in 'ere. F...... mate of mine wasn't f...... holdin' on tight a' f...... nuff. F...... truck goes over a f...... bump an' 'e goes straight out the f...... back an' lands on 'is f...... 'ead. Poor f.....!'

We held on. Leaning out of the back, we could see Mount Kenya proud above the forests, white glaciers shining in the sun. We'd be up there tomorrow.

They dropped us at Naro Moru, and we walked down to the Lodge where we used some of our few remaining shillings to hire two sleeping bags, a jacket and a couple of ice axes. The Lodge sits at about 5,000 feet, the same altitude as the roadhead on Kilimanjaro. So a long hard walk from here to one of the camps on Mount Kenya would be excellent training. We started at midday, and we walked hard for the 13 miles up to the Park Entrance. We got there at 5 pm, only to be told by the armed sentry on the gate that it could be dangerous to continue, because the wild animals—particularly the buffalo—would all be coming out of the jungle for the night and moving along the trail.

We looked at our watches: one hour till darkness. The sentry said that if we could get to the next camp, the Met Station, in one hour, we should be all right. As we left, he reminded us about the buffaloes.

'Very dangerous, especially when there's just one. Be careful.'

From the Park Gate the trail starts to climb up through dense equatorial forest. Monkeys watched us from the trees, and through a window in the wall of juicy green vegetation we caught a glimpse of the plains far below us, tinted in blue-grey haze. The sun, large, low and pillowed by clouds on the horizon was radiating wan shafts of dusky light towards us. In the quiet cool of the evening, away from bouncing trucks and searing desert heat, it was a moment of supreme tranquillity and contrast to the previous few days.

Then we met the buffalo.

I froze, borrowed a few expletives from our army friends of the morning, then asked Pete if we could go home. The thing was absolutely enormous, as big as a bus with a face like a hairy cow-pat; black and menacing with two of the biggest and sharpest looking horns that can ever have been attached to a mammal. It just stood there, right in the centre of the trail, staring. Pete, ever the optimist (I called him a suicidal maniac later), insisted we carry on and walk past the brute.

'It won't do anything if we don't frighten it' he told me.

'Look, the thing's as big as a locomotive. And it's got vicious spikes. All it's got to do is flick us with one of those and we'll be properly nobbled. I think we should climb a tree and wait for it to go away.' I looked around for trees to climb. There were plenty, but all had tall shiny trunks devoid of handholds.

Pete carried on walking, me trailing behind feeling very unhappy. When we got a few yards away, we scrambled down a bank, and attempted to bypass the animal, on all fours. Just as we drew level, and my heart was revving like a two-stroke about to seize, the buffalo stamped its front feet on the ground, shaking the earth and raising a cloud of dust, started towards us, then, inexplicably, turned around and plunged back into the jungle with a devastating crashing of splintering wood. For half a minute we knelt frozen whilst the beast charged through the trees like a rogue bulldozer. If I'd been Biggles I might have said something like 'Cripes, that was a close shave'. But this was 1984, and all that came to mind was 'Shittabrick!'

Above: Mists and rain in the ericaceous zone above the equatorial jungle reminded us fondly of family climbs in the Scottish mountains.
Below: By 10,000 feet the joke had worn a bit thin.
Right: We cycled through Alpine-like vegetation and across tumbling streams which split the rugged flanks of Mawenzi.

That night we were spared a bitterly cold night in the open, thanks to the hospitality of a group of British climbers. We left them before dawn the next morning, intent on getting as high as possible on the mountain by lunch-time. The air at 10,000 feet was chilly, and to keep warm, I tied a sleeping bag around me using a length of string. Our rations for the day were four maize cakes and half a jar of pineapple jam. 'All good training for Kilimanjaro,' I tried to convince myself as we trudged uphill with rumbling stomachs. We came into the Teleki Valley just after dawn, and made Mackinder's Camp at 13,000 feet, later in the morning.

By now clouds were boiling in the cauldron beneath the glaciers of Batian and Nelion, the twin peaks of Mount Kenya, and flurries of snow were whistling through the Camp. It's a spectacular place: from the rounded volcanic dome of Mount Kenya's lower slopes, a cluster of rock spires and precipitous grey walls soar 2,000 feet up to hanging ice. Features are named after the early climbing pioneers or relate to the area's geographical splendour: Shipton's Peak, Mackinder's Gendarme and Thomson's Flake rub shoulders with the Diamond Couloir and the Gate of Mists.

Above us we could see the hanging whiteness of the Lewis glacier, and the ice-field that Ados and I had crossed earlier in the year. Last February, we'd planned a quick attempt at climbing Nelion and Batian, a two-day rock climb which starts on the glacier. We'd been travelling as light as possible, and only had a tin of sardines, some biscuits and maize cakes to last us three days. Not far up the climb, altitude sickness struck in a devastating fashion, and we had to beat a hasty retreat to the valley below. This time we'd be better acclimatised. Pete and I were both feeling strong, and were hardly noticing the effects of altitude, a good omen for Kilimanjaro. With the wind freezing our ears, we snapped a 'high-point' photograph, turned and bolted for the valley. By midnight we were back in Nairobi.

Base Camp and the Team

Bar and her husband Rod have lived in Nairobi for several years now, and have two sons. Rod has spent most of his life in Kenya and both are adept at getting around red tape. They provided the control centre and headquarters for our expedition and the team got together in dribs and drabs a few days before Christmas.

Bar gave up a bedroom for Pete and I to organise the equipment, and it wasn't until we'd filled the room up to waist level and camped in it for a couple of days that we realised there was another occupant, Steve from Essex, who had been shipwrecked on the Seychelles while on a round-the-world sailing trip, and was now based in Nairobi building sailing dinghies. He proved as efficient at locating bicycle chain lubricant and border permits for our trip as he was at caulking a forepeak.

Michèle had arrived in Nairobi that afternoon, having had some exciting solo adventures. She had journeyed on public transport, by truck and on foot, to the bush village of Nzeluni where she had taught English for one year in 1978. She had been one of the first foreign teachers in the new school and had been given responsibility as overseer to the girls' dormitory and as deputy headmistress. She takes up her story:

> Nzeluni was in so many ways just as I remembered it with two dusty red
> tracks leading into the marketplace surrounded by a cluster of homes. As

I walked the last three hours from the roadhead into the village, the bush telegraph spread ahead of me and the two Mukamba sisters came out to meet me. Frederick Mutinga was waiting at the school. He's the odd-job man and his warm smile has not changed since he was a Form 2 pupil seven years ago.

When I woke the next morning, changes became more apparent to me. There are now two motor cars and the naive painting on the outside wall of the *chai* house has been changed from wild animals to women in bikinis. The derelict sheds in which I taught are disused and numerous new buildings stand proudly beside them. All the stones for the foundations were collected by the girls after their homework was completed at night. Cement, windows, corrugated iron and other building materials were bought from outside the area and have left the school a crippling debt. There have been great problems getting funds and a new headmaster has been installed.

Worse than the financial situation, the school suffered badly from the last two years of drought. Food was scarce, and water had to be bought from vendors in the neighbouring villages over 20 kilometres away. The pupils carried it back on their heads in large metal *karais*.

This hardship has not affected the traditional generous *kamba* welcome, which I was shown when I sprang a visit on Phoebe in her home. We had taught together and now she has two children, one of whom bobbed up and down on her back whilst she washed the clothes. We ate *ugali* and beans and in the kitchen I spotted a tin of Kimbo, the shiny white lard used for cooking. It's as common in the shops as Coca-cola and it always reminds me of some of the similes which the pupils had suggested in answer to a question: 'Describe your ideal companion.' One boy thought . . . 'She will have thighs like Kimbo', whilst others offered 'lips as smooth as bubblegum' . . . or . . . 'breasts like two surprised squirrels in the road.'

Kate and Maggie had been warming-up for the big climb by taking a train down to the sweltering heat of the Indian Ocean, where they spent a few days on the coast north of Mombasa, staying in local huts and being ravaged by mosquitoes. When they returned to Nairobi they found a mountain of tasks waiting. A shopping list as long as a lizard (big African variety) had to be ticked off, and this meant scouring the local stores for items that were often hard to find. Bit by bit a heap of things like flour, string, candles, matches, torch batteries, sugar and chocolate piled up on Bar's verandah. The chocolate was the single most important food item on the list. Both Dick and I knew from past experience that 'choccy-bars' are one of the few things that remain palatable above 15,000 feet. As the bulging bag of chocolate was deposited in Bar's freezer to prevent it from melting in the balmy heat, I made a mental note that, of all the equipment and provisions we were taking, we mustn't forget the choccy. The other thing we needed was our co-leader Dick who had been spending his time sampling the snows of Scotland.

Above: Carrying the loads on our backs rather than in panniers attached to the bikes made a big difference to our agility over tricky terrain.

Below: Kate (left of photo) was no stranger to exotic lands, having travelled in the Far East, but this was her first proper mountain and first visit to Africa.

Above: Trying to tie a foam sleeping-mat to a frame-tube for shoulder padding. *Above right:* At Horombo, making last adjustments to wheel-bearings before dumping the heavier tools and pushing on to higher altitudes. *Below left:* With her previous zoological studies in Zimbabwe, Maggie was our walking encyclopaedia on flora and fauna. *Below right:* Pete declared special interests: fell-walking, cycling, taking good photographs, home-brew—but not necessarily in that order.

(Dick's diary, 23 December 1984. Above Africa on London to Nairobi flight.) Dawn is breaking over Ethiopia. The entire landscape comprises groups of dry brown hills lined by long-dead stream-beds. Among this scrubland there are some of the thousands of Africans suffering poverty, disease and starvation in the drought. The sun is squeezing above the horizon: round and red.

The stewardess has offered a choice of drinks. Water is not available unless you want it iced, fizzy, or with lemon. The aeroplane drones on and I'm again looking out of the window.

We are crossing at 36,000 feet and 400 mph into the north-west of Kenya. From a communist-influenced to a capitalist-influenced country. No geographical boundary. The same poor hungry people everywhere. A drought has no political constraints.

Way off to the east, out of the port windows, is Wajir. Did Nick and Pete get there? Is a windmill to pump water the best way of helping? Or will it lure the nomads from the semi-desert around and make them dependent on the village?

The long shadows across the valleys are shortening rapidly as the sun rises. I can see occasional dusty tracks wriggling among the hills. The semi-desert stretches endlessly west towards the Sahara. A couple of isolated mountain groups are coming up as silhouettes in the east. There is Lake Turkana. And somewhere close is Lodhwar.

I first came here with Ados 11 years ago. Uncle Bill left us £300 each. We spent it all on a ticket to East Africa. Did the game parks and tourist beaches. All good fun but disappointingly predictable. With one week left, we stuck out our necks and boarded a truck to the remote north-west. We found ourselves in Lodhwar. Brushwood shelters and a few ramshackle huts. Acacias and thorn-bushes. Mostly rock and sand and sparse tussocks of grass.

For the first time in our lives we saw primitive people, some dressed in no more than a loin cloth, one or two older men in nothing at all, others with a simple brown blanket thrown over their shoulders. Women with their hair in intricate plaits and a heavy yoke of neck ornaments.

Such is Lodhwar. Our initiation into the ways and truths of the world and her people. The single most important adventure of our early lives. A lot of water has passed under the bridge since then. Climbing, travelling, cycling, university. Ados has worked in Saudi Arabia and I've worked in South America. We've climbed in the Alps, the Atlas, the Appalachians and Andes. Ados and I did the expedition 'Running the Himalayas.'

All the time we've remembered the Lodhwar Syndrome: to take a big risk on big returns. Always we believe it's a calculated gamble.

Now Nick and I are into a totally new adventure. For the first time in our lives (by 'our' I mean our little group of friends and relatives), other people expect results from this expedition. The only acceptable result is success. The mental pressure is intense. Gone are the free unrestricted excitements of Ados' Himalayan adventure. Everyone wants the action they saw from afar on 'Running the Himalayas'. I hope that Nick and I can pull it off.

Lake Turkana has passed below. I can't see Mount Kenya. The stewardess has just said 'Belts on. We'll be landing at Nairobi airport in fifteen minutes. The ground temperature is 26° above freezing. The sun is shining.' I wonder if she has looked out of the window.

Across the Great Divide

The Rift Valley is a couple of hours' drive north from Nairobi, and we set off soon after Dick had devoured a late breakfast. The area is comparatively dry, carpeted sometimes with scrub and dotted with volcanic cones. Sitting like a giant puddle in the bottom of the Rift Valley, is Lake Naivasha. West of its placid waters are the low ramparts of the Mau Escarpment, to the east, rising in a series of giant steps, the slope of the Rift Valley climbs up to the Aberdare Mountains. Part way up this slope is 'Trees,' a small house with a garden which, on 23 December 1984, could be seen strewn with pieces of Saracen ATB mountainbikes attended by bodies in various states of repose.

For the first time, the entire crew of 'Mountainbikes up Kilimanjaro' was in one place. Pete was still looking slightly dazed by the events of the past few days, and Dick, only in Kenya for a handful of hours so far, was raring to get the bikes in order.

All of the assembled throng tried the bikes. Just outside the gate was a steep tussocky grass hill, ideal for romping over with a mountainbike. And even the altitude, 8,000 feet, added to the value of these two days of work-outs. There were a number of modifications and adjustments to be made to the bikes. We experimented with different saddle heights, and moved the handlebars up and down. The more we rode them, the more we became convinced that we'd need to fit the super-low gears Dick had brought out with him.

(Dick) Greg Oxenham at Bike UK in London, had been very accommodating with my urgent request a few days earlier for 'ultra-low mountainbike sprockets, changers, cables and all the tools to fit them on.' He's an expert in tinkering with bikes and had been the one who'd fitted out the two machines Nick and I had used so successfully on the 14 Peaks in North Wales. Bike UK packaged up not only gears but spare inner tubes, puncture kits and brake levers. I collected them all in a mad panic just a few hours before getting on the plane for Nairobi.

In the sun at Trees, the inquisitive little fingers of Barrod's children 'JJ' and Adrian got to work on the packages. The two boys discovered that the 36-tooth rear sprocket made nice dents in Michèle's legs. Rodney, Pete and Steve soon found that it was easier to pull the rear wheel to pieces than to re-assemble it. A large spanner was needed. We searched all through the house, cleared out the shed and looked in the Land Rover bonnet. No luck. Jarrod, the housekeeper, came to our rescue when we showed him what we needed. He found a huge coarse file, gripped an undersize spanner between the jaws of his ancient vice, and ground it to fit.

The gear modifications were radical. We could now pedal up the steepest slopes outside 'Trees'. Rod, whose experience at 'tweaking' and racing rally-cars, was an inspirational force, lent all sorts of theories on hill-climbing and descending techniques. In a quest for the ultimate off-roader, he attacked the 'spare' bike, reversing the handlebars and sinking them right into the frame; lifting the saddle high for maximum power. I could imagine the stylist at Saracen wincing if he'd seen the result. Rod, Dick and I circuited the scrubby slopes for hours, practicing riding up vertical banks, and dropping the bikes over sharp edges. I came back from one of these with the first genuine 'Bicycles up Kilimanjaro' injury, a row of impressive holes

Above: Beyond the rain forest and the transition zone of the lower slopes there was the prospect of several hours' cycling before finding snow and ice that could be melted for drinking water.

Below: The trouble with being the front rider is that you always fall in the hole first.

in my leg caused by an over-the-handlebar plummet down a rock step. We still had a lot to learn.

A proving ride was planned for the next day. Rod, Dick and I would take the three bikes and attempt to ride them down the wall of the Rift Valley and through the bush to a farm owned by Rod's aunt. Kate, Maggie, Michèle, Pete and Steve the Boatbuilder would get up before dawn and climb Longonot, a 9,000 foot volcano. We'd all meet up at the farm in the afternoon.

(Dick's diary, 23 December 1984, Trees.) This is so exciting. At last we have ridden the mountainbikes in Africa. The Rift Valley might not be the same as the highest mountain but it's steep, rough and quite awe-inspiring. This is the sort of tussle with machines I've been waiting for. Now we'll find out how they handle. And how we can handle them.

'Make hay while the sun shines' goes the maxim, so we tested the bikes as far as our nerves would allow us. Rod and I went off pedalling around and around the scrub beyond Trees, waiting for Nick to get his derailleur sorted. We mastered a high-speed, stand-up, bounding technique for crossing clearings of coarse tussocky grass, and then went in search of tiny one or two-foot yumps to hop up and down. Nick appeared and attacked the yump with a vengeance, but didn't get enough wheel-lift and stopped dead as though he'd ridden into a brick wall. All good experience. We were learning fast.

The three of us set off together down the scarp face of the Rift Valley. It turned into a really hairy tussle through tangled thorn bushes and blocky igneous boulders which poked through dry broken soil. I started by skidding off a loose corner into a low bush and meeting face-to-face with a bees' nest. Not a word of commiseration from either my cousin or brother-in-law who both whooped past at speed. I caught them again when we had to lift the bikes over a group of boulders, and this gave us a chance to exchange our marvels at the control that was possible at breakneck speed. Pedalling again, Rod led away, pulled hard on his front brake, took a purler front dive and yelled enthusiastically 'These cantilevers are fantastic!' Nick and I dashed past, with Nick gaining ground, skimming over the knobbliest lumps till he lost it on a two-foot rock-step and shoulder-charged a thorn-bush.

We were having a lot of fun. Each 'mishap' was an excuse to tell the others how 'our' style had been 'good' or 'nearly perfect'. Our skills improved in leaps and bounds.

We were like schoolboys who'd just been given new racers for Christmas. Below the rock-face we struck off across the scrub, bouncing the bikes through grassy dells and powering them with their front wheels lifted over rounded humps. A Masai herdsman, sitting with his spear by a tree, watched wide-eyed as we bumped past and disappeared into a patch of dense thorn. A herd of zebra scattered before us.

The course of a dried-up river provided several interesting little micro-terrain problems. We were all becoming adept at lifting the front wheel up a step, but the problem always seemed to be to get the rear wheel to follow. Many times I'd be poised on the lip of a gully, nearly making the top, but, at the last moment toppling sideways.

As well as testing the bikes, this 'proving ride' was intended also to resolve the problem of how best to carry our luggage up Kilimanjaro. The choice was between panniers attached to the backs of the bikes, or rucksacks attached to the backs of the riders. An afternoon in the Rift valley convinced that the latter option was by far the best—at low altitudes anyway. Panniers on a bucking mountainbike, I quickly found, destroy the critical balance of the machine. Put the weight on your back, and the bike remains light and lively; far more manoeuvrable over difficult ground. The weight of a rucksack, bound securely to the rider's torso can be shifted forward or back, side-to-side, depending on the terrain. So rucksacks won the day, but we thought we'd take the panniers up 'Big K' 'just in case'.

It took three hours to reach the farm, navigating in part by the sun. The bikes had performed splendidly, and not even the giant thorns had managed to penetrate the tyres, which seemed armour-plated. We were exhausted, drenched in sweat and dehydrated. We had a colourful collection of cuts and bruises, and a couple of potentially more serious problems. The muscles along the insteps of our feet were tight and sore; walking was difficult. Several hours of balancing on the balls of our feet, pushing hard and then relaxing on the pedals, and the use of our feet as human shock-absorbers, had stretched un-trained ligaments. The outer fleshy parts of the palms of our hands were raw and blistered from the constant battle to steer bucking machines over rutted ground. We'd have to wear gloves.

The Longonot contingent arrived an hour later, covered from head to toe in a cake of dust, and full of volcano adventures. It had been scorchingly hot on the climb, but they'd managed to complete a traverse of the entire crater, and were all claiming supreme altitude acclimatisation and fitness. Michèle had a go at redressing the healthy balance by trying to ride one of the mountainbikes over a children's see-saw, falling off at the highest point and landing on her face. Beer and tea quenched thirsts; we consumed a memorable hot curry on a hot day, packed up the bikes and headed for Nairobi. It was Christmas Eve.

Christmas Day came by like the one scheduled stop on a particularly long and exciting train journey. For 24 hours the frenetic adventuring was interrupted by more convivial activities: breakfast of fresh mangoes and pancakes, then to the cathedral for a hand-clapping carol-singing Christmas service, followed by swimming outdoors and Christmas lunch. Normally immodest appetites were swelled by the thought that this might be the last proper meal for quite some time.

Trouble

(Dick's diary, Boxing Day 1984.) We left for Tanzania the next morning in the Land Rover, three mountainbikes tied on the roof along with jerrycans of spare petrol, and six people jammed inside with a multitude of rucksacks. White faces peering out of the windows. Black kids wave outside. Two little girls in Sunday School dresses carry firewood on their heads. Women wear bright coloured kangas and have cheerful round faces. Teenage youths flash gaudy shirts and flared trousers. A huge black truck with a heavy trailer is tilted over on the side of the road and three beefy mechanics dressed in overalls covered in oil are lying in the ditch manhandling a lump of metal the size of an aircraft engine. A group of children watch.

Rich green maize fields, dark mango trees, and leafy avocado with waxy sheen. Flimsy coffee bushes, dense banana trees and a swarm of flies. Traditional single room mud huts and modern breeze-block bungalows. A ruined car, a fallen telegraph pole and a cloud of black smoke from a labouring over-laden truck. A boy in grey shorts with a torn blue shirt on the verge beside a box of tomatoes he's selling. An old man pedals by on a big black bicycle built like a juggernaut.

We bowled across the plains in high spirits. Michèle and Kate sang; Maggie told of her adventures in Malawi. This was it. At last, we were really on our way. Dick instigated a game to help pass the time. For every different species of animal or bird you could spot, you scored a point. Within three miles Dick had claimed a herd of goats, 2 giraffes, 9 Thomson's Gazelles, 7 Wildebeest, the entire population of a village market, a Malibu stork and a dead dog (disallowed after much debate on the grounds that more than half of it was eaten away), bringing his points total to 264. No one else had got more than 10, and I had yet to see anything new moving at all. The trouble with competing with Dick is that he's always worked out how to win, before the game starts.

(Dick) We searched for one important sight. We knew that somewhere approximately south-east should be Big-K. From an 11-year memory and the dreams of the past 11 weeks, I imagined it huge and white, soaring above the clouds. From 100 miles away, I looked up at 10 degrees to spot the mountain. I fully believed it to be there. Luckily it wasn't, because that would have made Kilimanjaro nearly 100,000 feet high; four times as high as Everest, and too much for us on foot, let alone by bike!

We dreamt on, with visions of our grand mountain, but by mid-afternoon the clouds had closed in and we were obviously not going to see our target for a while.

Somebody got hungry, and pulled out a couple of loaves and an enormous plastic tub of peanut butter. As we munched we worried about the possibility of hitting more bureaucratic problems at the border between Kenya and Tanzania. It was the last hurdle we had to cross. After that it would be plain sailing—or rather riding.

The border at Namanga is little more than a loose collection of shacks clustered around the two police posts, one for each country, about a hundred yards apart. Behind the tin roofs is the bush rising up to low, smooth volcanic hills. It's a very hot place. We'd rehearsed our story on the way down, and had plenty of 'props' to help us talk our way through. In Nairobi we'd been told that we'd need an export/import licence for both the Land Rover and the bikes. So we'd collected an impressive file of forms, all filled in neatly. One form was required not to be in duplicate, or even triplicate, but seventeen-icate! Michèle tackled the men in uniform, explaining that we were visiting Tanzania on holiday, and that we planned to do a bit of cycling round and about 'while we're in your beautiful country'. It worked. After relieving us of enough Kenyan shillings to keep all the border guards in beer for a year, the major-domo of the outfit waved us through.

(Dick) Euphoria was still with us when we caught our first sight of Kilimanjaro, a squat shadow in the clouds, indistinct, but nevertheless there. Its main bulk is a large dome rising steeply at first out of the East African plains and then levelling off at 15,000 feet. Out of the dome sticks the impressive snow-capped volcanic cone of Kibo summit at 19,340 feet. To one side are the jagged black fingers of Mawenzi, the little sister, at 16,889 feet.

An hour after nightfall, we pulled in to the Marangu Hotel, an old colonial-style establishment run by Mrs Gordon-Bennett. We'd been told to report here to arrange for porters and to pay the necessary trekking charges. After ten hours of travelling, it was good to stop, and we were looking forward to a cup of tea and hopefully an enthusiastic welcome from the locals. After all, it couldn't be every day that people turn up in Marangu to ride bicycles up the highest mountain in Africa. Dick and I went inside, and were met by a grey-haired lady who asked our business.

'Well, we're just dropping by to make arrangements for tomorrow. We want to leave at dawn, and start our ride up the mountain.'

'What do you mean, "start your ride"? Do you have motor-cycles?'

'No, no, these are bicycles. We want to cycle them up Kilimanjaro.'

'Well it's out of the question. You're not allowed to do that. Two Australians came with bicycles one month ago and were turned away. I'm sorry. If you don't believe me, go and ask Mr Nassari, the National Park Head Warden. He'll tell you.'

I was stunned. Dick said nothing. What an absolute foul-up. Why the hell hadn't we checked on this before? The others greeted the news with silence. We got back in the vehicle, and Pete drove slowly on up the road. Out of the window I just caught a tantalising view of Kili, dark and rounded like a giant Christmas pudding with its summit snows lit by the moon, gleaming white like a topping of cream, taunting us. Before, it had looked so close. Now it seemed a million miles away.

Let the Game Commence

That moment of nausea that comes with complete disaster wasn't a new sensation. There was the time in northern Scotland when we realised we were committed to an exposed night in bivouac sacks on the Corrag Buidh Pinnacles when we couldn't get any further down a snow gully in the dark; the micro-second in the Portuguese mountains when I realised I wasn't going to get around the hairpin; the time when Klon peeled off a rock wall and all his belays popped out.

'Bicycles up Kilimanjaro' had itself already had its fair share of nervy hurdles: the plane tickets which had only been acquired at the very last moment, the excess luggage frightener at Heathrow, and the customs man at Nairobi; Dick being told he wasn't booked on the flight after all; the Wajir episode; the buffalo; getting the bikes past the Tanzanian customs; the Land Rover skidding out of control on the wet road just south of the border. With each difficulty, we'd been saved either by the intervention of luck or a Good Samaritan. After coming so far, we surely couldn't be halted now?

(Dick) Nothing was going to stop us now. Nick and I had got bikes, equipment, support team and I.T. involvement this far and by hook or by crook we'd get up that mountain. We climbed back into the stuffy Land Rover. The other four were still chirpy about our arrival but we soon dampened their spirits. After explaining our predicament, we had some serious thinking to do.

Several alternatives presented themselves. We could knock on the door of the National Park Headquarters and ask if they would change their minds about bicycles. We could pay our entry fees as walkers and try to smuggle the bicycles in pieces past the Park gate. Kate suggested charging past the officials in top gear and ignoring the yells. Maggie wondered if we should pack up and try again next year. Michèle wanted a confrontation. Nick and I wondered about forgetting this route and going for the other side of the mountain. We could even abandon Kilimanjaro and go for Mount Kenya.

The plan which we finally selected as having most potential and certainly most fun was to go for direct confrontation. We drove gently over to the Nat Park HQ. No one spoke. The others stayed in hiding, whilst Nick and I headed through the darkness to the only lodge with lights. This turned out to be the bar and Nick and I entered with bated breath.

Inside the room, the tables were busy with porters, guides and Tanzanian Park personnel. We were clearly out of place. We found Mr Nassari, a smart trim man, leaning on the bar. Our first move to break the ice was to offer a beer which he firmly declined. I realised that it could be a long discussion and the whole affair eventually dragged on tensely for two hours.

He didn't know we were the two eccentrics who wanted to cycle up his mountain and we had no intention of telling him for a while. We chatted casually at first about general schedules and team members. He quickly realised that we were a little 'odd' (I kicked Nick's shins to stop him laughing) and then since we offered to promote the National Park for tourism, he called his deputy over. We fixed up porters and guides and fees for this expedition which was referred to as 'unusual' without specifying why. Then, when he had heard all about I.T., and the matter was virtually settled, I casually dropped in a mention that we would be using bicycles.

If Mr Nassari had been frivolous enough to drink beer he would have spattered it all over the floor. As far as he was concerned it was all right to organise long expeditions, charity expeditions, photographic expeditions or even 'odd' expeditions. But bicycles were another matter. One more hour of gentle explanation and persuasion were needed to calm him down. We did so well that he ended up as enthusiastic as ourselves and elected us honorary 'Friends of Kilimanjaro'.

While Dick was discussing the value of ecological research in the tropics with Mr Nassari, I was holding my breath in the background, desperately willing the Park Warden to say the right things. He did, and after what seemed an eternity, we walked out of the bar, Dick holding in his hand a single sheet of white paper—our passport to the mountain. I was bursting with joy: nothing, absolutely nothing, could stop us now. I wanted to scream with delight. Dick was grinning from ear to ear. 'Mmm, you did rather well in there,' I said as we sprinted out into the dark. We burst into laughter and then stopped and walked calmly and straight-faced up to the Land Rover.

The others had waited in virtual silence for two hours and were despondent and anxious to hear what Mr Nassari had told us.

'Bad news I'm afraid,' I said with a long face as we got near. The four of them were grouped around the front of the vehicle, Maggie hunched up in the cold and sitting on the bumper.

'A bit of a pity really,' continued Dick, 'we've been told it's out of the question to go up Kili. It's not allowed. There is an alternative way up the mountain, which starts in the jungle 70 miles from here. We could drive there now, and see if we can get permission tomorrow morning to try that route. How much petrol is there Pete?'

Pete, his face crossed with anguish at the thought of 70 miles of dirt roads at night with insufficient petrol, on top of the 10 hours we'd already done that day, leant over the dashboard.

Dick carried on:' 'course the trouble with this other route is that it's got a vertical ice-wall near the top; I'm not sure we've got the right gear to tackle it'. Pulling himself out of the cab, Pete muttered doomily 'That's serious'. He doesn't list severe ice-climbing among his favourite occupations. 'What are we going to do?'

'Well, tell you what, [Dick let out a despondent sigh] let's go over to the bar and have a hot meal [he spoke quicker and broke into a smile]. Mr Nassari says it will be on the table in ten minutes [excited tone]. Then we'll go to the room he's booked us for the night and get a good kip [Dick was now ecstatically babbling]. And in the morning we'll show the guard on the gate our permission to go up the mountain [Dick waved the piece of paper] and by lunchtime tomorrow we'll be at . . .'

'You stinking swines. You complete and utter heroes.' The expedition photographer started leaping up and down hugging everybody.

It took an hour to stow all the gear and the bikes in our tiny room. There were three sets of bunk beds around the walls, and these were used as shelves for sorting equipment. Dick and I checked over the three bikes; the plan was for Pete to use the spare machine. The three of us would set off early next morning, get as high as we could by 11 am, take *The Sunday Times* photos, then return as fast as possible to Marangu Gate and hand the material over to Mary-Anne Fitzgerald. The pictures should, if the plan worked, arrive in London the next morning. It would mean that Dick and I had to do the first day of ascent twice, but (we assured each other) it would be good training. While Pete, Dick and I were out playing in the jungle, Kate, Maggie and Michèle would pack the expedition rucksacks and organise the porters.

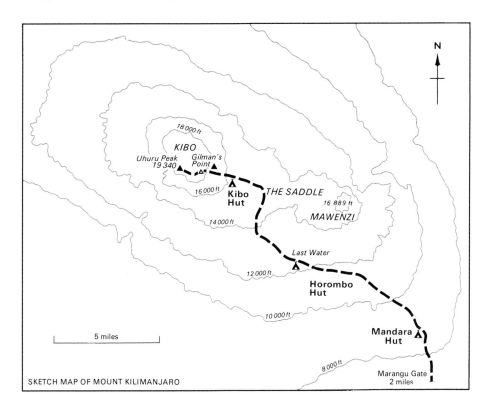

SKETCH MAP OF MOUNT KILIMANJARO

We spread out the map for a final route check. We'd reckoned on taking between 4 and 6 days to reach the summit. Day 1 would see us through the jungle to Mandara Hut. On Day 2 we'd leave the jungle and ride up to Horombo Hut at about 12,500

55

feet. From then on we'd be into the zone of 'thin air' and would be suffering increasingly from altitude sickness. Day 3 would find us climbing up across the lower flank of Mawenzi, out onto a broad plateau to the foot of the 3,000-foot volcanic cone of Kilimanjaro's main peak: Kibo. From a camp at the bottom of this cone near Kibo Hut at 15,000 ft we'd assess our progress, and use Day 4 and 5 to make the final climb up to the rim of the crater and along to Uhuru Peak, Kilimanjaro's summit. The round trip to the top and back totalled about 80 kilometres of cycling.

(Dick's diary, late night, Boxing Day, Marangu Gate.) Big day tomorrow. Kili here we come. Just got to pack our rucksacks. Lots of junk here—like we've transported 72 St John St wholesale to Africa. Goodness knows how we'll get it up the mountain. Got the girls to sort out the porters. It's not a job which Nick or I fancied doing. Too much hassle and haggling. I've no idea how you decide which porters are going to be good. How big is the load they can carry? Do we have to provide their food? How much do they cost? Do you have to give tips? Good Luck, girls.

There was scarcely room to move in the hut. Pete had spread out all his camera gear, and was agonising over which lenses to take and how best to pack them for easy access. Dick had decided that the headset on his bike was too loose, and was wrestling with a huge adjustable spanner. It was 2.30 in the morning before we filled our packs and finished the last adjustment to our mountainbikes. We were up again three hours later. While the other three slept, Pete, Dick and I had a 'breakfast' of bread and pineapple jam. The sky was still dark, and we stealthily pushed the bikes out into the night air. It seemed scarcely believable that our tyres were at last rolling on Kilimanjaro. It was fifteen minutes before dawn on 27 December 1984. 'About bloody time' whispered Dick.

Quietly into the Trees

(Dick's diary, 27 December 1984.) I never thought we'd see an end to the organisational problems. Quite a battle in itself. It's taken us two months to get the show on the road, but that's still light years faster than many big expeditions. Start at 05.45 hrs this morning. The REAL start. We're on the mountain now. We'll be unstoppable. No one can take us away from the mountain now, no-one can drag us from our goal. It's all down to us and our ability. I'm convinced that between us we've got the experience. I know that I can go to that height, Nick can definitely handle these bikes, but can we both do both? Will the bikes hold together?

We carried the bikes past the 'Gate' and two sentries standing wrapped to their ears in heavy khaki greatcoats, rifles propped at their sides. There was no point in waking them unnecessarily. Out of sight around the first bend, we lowered the bikes to the ground and began pedalling.

(Dick) 'Crunch. A horrific grinding noise came from my transmission. The pedals jerked forward but my bike stopped dead. I gingerly dismounted and explored the gear mechanism. The chain had slipped across several sprockets, not completely catching on any, because I'd knocked the derailleur into a higher gear without turning the wheels.

Luckily no damage. A good lesson. It mustn't happen again.

I grabbed hold of the chain and lifted it back onto the sprockets. Dirty bicycle grease all over my hands. We had only come 100 yards, not even cycling! I remounted. Already Nick was way ahead. I hammered hard to catch him but ended up out of breath, well-warmed and feeling a little out of condition. We were only 6,000 feet above sea-level. It could only get harder.

From the dark jungle on each side of the track came the sounds of waking wildlife: the chattering of birds, odd shrieks, hoots and howls. The air was quite still, making the rasping from our unpractised lungs seem unnaturally loud. At first the track was wide and firm enough to take a four-wheel drive vehicle. It climbed steeply and it wasn't long before we were fumbling, with early-morning clumsiness, for the low gears.

I was boiling over with heat build-up inside all my thermal clothing. After 15 minutes I stopped and stripped down to a T-shirt while Dick caught up. For just a moment as Dick approached he was silhouetted in a gap in the trees against the lightening eastern sky, a solitary cyclist etched in black, hunched and panting. As the track narrowed and steepened, the trees closed in over our heads till we were riding through a dim tunnel of foliage. Fronds and lianas brushed our elbows, and the tyres began to slip on damp rocks and patches of mud washed down from the banks. Short, sharp rock steps came more frequently, and we had to attack these out of the saddle, lifting the front wheel then powering the back wheel up the rise. Daylight crept up on us unnoticed.

(Dick) After the first easy mile or so we entered proper jungle, and the surface alternated between glossy rocks and sticky mud. The continuous riding sections of hundreds of yards at a time became reduced to 20 or 30 yard battles terminated by bouncing slides on chunky rocks the size of footballs, or uncontrollable wheel-spin on the steeper slippery bed-rock. Surprisingly, mud did not seem a problem yet. The thin film of water looked skiddy on foot, but our big knobbly Canyon Express tyres bit through to take firm hold.

We had started the day wearing a full complement of riding gear: long socks and Brasher boots, our Berghaus salopettes, thermal long-sleeved vest and T-shirt, topped by both the inner thermal layer of our 'wonder-jackets' and the outer Goretex layer too. On our backs we had the Karrimor Hot Route sacs, containing Black's waterproof trousers, gloves, goggles, balaclava, compass, head-torch, bivouac bag and food for the day.

By the time we reached a sign saying '1½ Hours to Mandara' Pete was losing patience with the effort of trying to ride the bike and take photos at the same time. At a bend in the track, where it wriggled up a boulder slope, he slipped sideways for the umpteenth time, and cast a longing eye at a ravine which looked just the right size to accommodate a mountainbike flung from a great height. So the spare bike was ditched, hidden in the jungle beneath a canopy of broad wet leaves. We could pick it up later and take it back to Marangu Gate. 'There's no way this machine's going to help me get up this mountain; I can go quicker on foot.' Dick and I set out to prove Pete the Disbeliever wrong.

There was nobody else out on the trail at this early hour, and it was exhilarating to have the world to ourselves. As we gained height, the vegetation changed. Drapes of frilly ferns now hung from the trees of this exciting arboretum, and the path, in places just a foot wide, slithered through undergrowth that flicked against the spokes as we teetered past. There were a couple of narrow log bridges spanning fast brooks, and we found our first quagmire.

(Dick) Higher still, maybe 7,500 feet above sea-level, though it's difficult to tell one's position because the trees were too thick to take any bearings, the path got muddy. True jungle; not a rock in sight. The only knobbles on the ground were the knuckles of tree roots poking through to knock us off balance. They were a menace, because rubber tyres just cannot grip smooth wet wood, and my bike kept sliding off sideways, upending me in the mud. The only method I could find to get over the roots (barring chickening out and carrying the bike) was to approach head-on, at right-angles to the root, and hoick the handlebars hard to lift the front wheel over, or at least onto the root, then allow the bike to roll over onto firmer mud on the other side before turning the pedals a fraction then slinging my weight forward to encourage the rear end to come over in a straight line . . . rarely successful.

Late in the morning we came temporarily out of the trees and found ourselves on a broad patch of hummocky grass and heather spread over the crest of a ridge. It was a supremely satisfying moment: the first pause we'd had all day, and we'd come far enough already that the clouds were swelling and breaking on the green jungle some way below. Even the sun was trying to shine on us, through another level of higher-flying cloud above our heads. Sandwiched between a floor and ceiling of white, it all felt cosy, and we scrambled down a bank to find a sheltered spot for eating, and for writing the report for *The Sunday Times*. Dick and I took turns at adding paragraphs to a couple of sheets of A4 notepaper. We'd come far enough that morning to claim we'd truly got to grips with the mountain. We snacked on bread and dates, followed by a sesame seed bar for nibbles.

We reckoned that we could not be more than an hour below Mandara Hut, where we aimed to camp for the night. A plan for the day was formulated: while Pete stayed up on the mountain looking after the two bikes, Dick and I would return to the bottom (collecting the spare bike on the way) with the report and film, then climb back up again later in the afternoon. It seemed like a lot of extra exercise.

We left Pete sunbathing in his bush cradle, with the parting shot, 'Look after the bikes!'

And the Rains Came

Full of energy, we ran back down the trail. We'd agreed that I should pick up the spare bike, while Dick would run all the way with the newspaper despatch. It was vital we handed it over to Mary-Anne by 1 pm, if she was going to reach Nairobi in time for the evening plane. Not surprisingly, the descent turned out to be a race.

By the time I'd extricated the bike from its jungle hiding place, Dick had disappeared from sight, leaping and bounding down the rocks of the trail. I was determined not to let him get to the bottom first, partly because if he did, it would be a serious indictment of the mountainbike's descending ability; and partly because it wasn't one of the rules of the game to let the other win at anything.

It was the fastest I'd ever taken a bike downhill on rocks; the tyres were hard and bouncy, and I catapulted over the stones and roots, barely in control, pedalling like fury on any of the gentler slopes. What baulked a descent that would otherwise have been super-sonic were the sections of vertical rock which forced me to leap off and lift the machine for metres at a time. Each dismount lost me precious seconds. But I knew the last mile would be very much faster for me than Dick; I was banking on his tiring at just the point where I could accelerate and cruise past him on the line.

It wasn't to be. Just around a blind bend I met a family of baboons sauntering across the track. Rodney had warned that their attentions can be as evil as the appearance of their bright red backsides. Out of graciousness I felt unable to disturb the tranquillity of their post prandial perambulations, so waited patiently out of sight till they'd slipped into the bush.

Dick beat me by four minutes. When I arrived at Marangu Gate, he was chatting to Michèle, with a look of total calm. I walked over to him, trying to mask an expression which would give away the fact that I was wiped out by the ride.

'What was it like to ride?' he asked.

'Very pleasant really; just cruised down, stopping here and there. It seemed a pity to rush through all that beautiful scenery. Saw a family of baboons. Stopped for a drink and so on.' Those few words used up what little oxygen I had left, and I finished the sentence bent double, pretending to tie a boot-lace, while hoovering in a draught of air that stirred the leaves on the ground.

Dick's voice penetrated the rushing in my ears:

'Yeah, I did hang around a while to see if you were coming, but you didn't so I reckoned you'd had to fix the bike or something.'

(Dick) Life is sometimes just one big game. We discuss our plans and intentions objectively, exploring the pros and cons and balancing hardship, suffering and agony against the pleasures and prospects. However whenever we get to the action we degenerate into a 3rd XV scrum and our schooltime playground battles get the better of us. Just as Nick risked life and limb on that bicycle descent in order to beat me, I pulled out all the stops and hammered down on foot. I judged the distance from top to bottom, measuring my pace for the first section to stay a good distance ahead, then switched up to absolute flat out sprint for the final open stretch praying that I could hold on to the lead. I arrived at Marangu Gate hot, flustered and victorious. When Nick arrived he looked at his watch. We'd made the 4 mile, 2,000 feet descent in 29 and 33 minutes respectively.

Constant diary-writing is hard work but it's worth it in the end. Events can pass and be forgotten so quickly. I like to try to capture the mood and sensations of the moment. Emotions are as transient as the clouds around Kili. Like blizzards in the Arctic they are not always good. I reckon that if anyone reads any of my diary then they must realise that it records the emotions of the moment with no attempt to cover up any ill feeling or malice. They must realise that I'm the same as everyone else, and I can and will change my thoughts and feelings with time; be it two minutes, two days or two years.

It was warm and sunny and midday at Marangu Gate. Kate and Maggie were eager to set off up the trail with their bulging backpacks. Michèle was arguing with Mr Zablon about fees for entering the park. I wandered off to remove the derailleur from the spare bike so that we could take it with us up the mountain in case of our own ones packing up. Dick disappeared to write his diary.

(Dick's diary, 27 December 1984) My birthday! Nick seems more seriously intent on the grand overview of this 'Bicycles up Kilimanjaro' than me. I'm perhaps more light-hearted. Nick looks fifteen yards ahead on the trail and seems to be planning which line to take and which gear to use, while I'm messing about with the little knots of mud and clusters of flowers under my wheels. His intention would appear to be to complete the expedition to the best of his ability, and if there's any fun to be had along the way, that's a bonus. To me the aim is merely to get us plus two bikes up to the crater rim, and then to try our damnedest to cycle up to the summit. For me the journey should be as much fun as possible, and the serious work begins when we get back home to start the fund-raising drive for I.T.

Nick's view is altogether reasonable because he has been more completely submerged by this project than I have over the past few weeks. Indeed, has been out here visiting Wajir and training on Mount Kenya while I've been comfortable in the BP office in Aberdeen looking down microscopes at 200 million year old shallow marine sediments. This challenge on Kilimanjaro is merely an adventure for me in between my work, while for Nick it is an expedition on which his work depends.

(Dick) The cost has escalated ludicrously in the past few weeks. Initially we calculated a couple of airfares plus a little pocket money. About £1,000. However there are endless incidentals to pay for: telephones, postage, travelling, food, insurance, etc. Nick and I are paying all Pete's expenses so that he concentrates hard on the photography and so that Nick and I retain copyright on the photos. The girls are paying their own fares. The park fees totalled over £500, and Nick and I are out of pocket to the tune of £3,500. Expensive for a holiday, but good value if we raise funds for I.T.

One might suspect that it is less important to me that we get to the top. However I think we are both desperate to succeed. We will both pull out our last efforts to make it, even if we end up crawling and dragging the bikes. We have the hope of the windpump for Wajir hanging on it, plus the old Crane drive to persevere through adversity.

All in all, Nick rode more than me this morning. We both had a good laugh and my mountainbike skills improved by leaps and bounds, while Nick wiped away the cobwebs of Big City frustration.

Nick battled over many more roots than me. He pedalled along single-handed in places, fending off lianas and branches. He would not be stopped until he was physically knocked, or skidded, off his bike. Then he lay sprawled in the path grimacing for a couple of seconds till climbing to his feet again and charging off for another attack. I took it in a wholly easier frame of mind. I rarely crashed onto the ground because I always measured my approach to dicey bike manoeuvres and was ready to thrust out with my feet whenever necessary. It is true that I got hot and sweaty, but I was never really shattered like Nick.

Nick truly enjoyed the morning; a chance to get his teeth into something meaty. I too enjoyed the morning; a chance to relax and have a bit of fun.

On the gravel of the car park, I laid out all the bike equipment we'd be taking. There was the spare derailleur (and the chain) I'd cannibalised off the third bike, a freewheel block, one spare tyre, two inner tubes, two duplicate sets of tools, including an adjustable wrench big enough to remove a freewheel block. Put in a bag it all felt horrendously heavy. The porters would be useful.

Michèle had been at work all morning discussing wages and pack loads with an assortment of registered guides, park officials and hangers-on. Dick had suggested she get 5 or 6 porters for the journey up, 3 for the journey down. Luckily Michèle never believes him and she decided that eight were needed and so set about fixing them up.

One of our eight porters.

(Dick's diary 27 December 84, Marangu Gate, Afternoon.) M's got them all organised. Of the 20 or so porters standing around, we apparently have 8. They're a motley crowd: tall and short; some thin and straggly, others wiry, several are real musclemen; there's old 'uns and young 'uns. The only common denominator is black skins and a jolly smile. They're happy because they are the lucky ones who now have a job for the next week. It's well-paid compared to the local farmers' earnings, but typically it's very underpaid in

absolute financial terms. In one hour at my desk at BP, I earn enough to hire both a man and his son for a day.

There is quite a battle to be hired for work. Each guide has his own favourite porters who are: 'my good friend', 'my brother-in-law's stepson', 'this poor man's mother is ill', 'he needs money for his daughter's school'. In the end it all comes down to those who are close by and ready and able to go immediately. Maggie and Kate had dragged the rucksacks into the fray as Michèle bartered and haggled with the officials for permits and prices. The porters made a grab for the best-looking rucksacks, and then the girls had the trouble of trying to make them into equal loads.

When finally our porters set off, with Maggie and Kate in advance, Michèle, Dick and I were still left with a pile of rucksacks to get up to Mandara before nightfall. It was a long trudge, and Dick and I were carrying two rucksacks each and a 2-gallon can of petrol for our stove. At 3.30 pm it started to drizzle, then rain. Fat rods of water belting down from the sky bending leaves and soaking us to the skin. It was also cold and by the time we fished out our waterproof Gemini jackets from the depths of our backpacks, the shivers had set in. It was difficult even to see through the torrents, and just staying upright on the slimy mud required concentration. Parts of the trail became gushing streams which washed over my boots. Somewhere in this dismal progress I left Dick and Michèle.

(Dick) We headed for shelter under a large leafy tree, and stood awash in mud while huge gobs of water dropped on our heads. A hunky figure strode up the trail with a beaming smile and huge yellow plastic cape draped over a mountain of gear on his back. Simon must be the strongest man in action on this mountain. He had a medium sized rucksack strapped onto the back of one of our large expedition sacs, a Karrimor Condor 85, the biggest they make. On top of this he had his own provisions for eight days and clothes to take him to 18,000 feet. He gave a brief nod, a handshake and then, without hesitation, he reached out for the man-sized pack with which Michèle was struggling, whisked it up on to the top of his already formidable load, and pressed on up the hill.

When I reached the clearing where we'd left Pete and the bikes earlier in the day, it was like coming home. Not surprisingly, Pete wasn't waiting in the rain for us; we'd agreed that if the weather broke (and it most decidedly had) Pete should leave the bikes hidden in the bush in an agreed spot, and go on himself to find shelter at Mandara Hut, which couldn't be more than an hour up the trail.

I dropped my packs on the trail, so that Dick would know I was in the area, and moved off into the bush to collect my bike. It wasn't there. I searched and searched, kicking away at the scrub and branches, lifting the undergrowth. There wasn't the slightest trace that either bike had ever been there. I stood, soaked and cold, working through in my mind all the possibilities: it was inconceivable that Pete should have taken them on up to Mandara; he knew how important it was for Dick and me to ride the whole way ourselves, and anyway, we'd specifically arranged that he should leave the bikes in the spot where we'd eaten elevenses and written *The Sunday Times* report. My mind kept coming back to one awful conclusion: that somebody had stumbled across the bikes quite by chance, recognised how valuable they were, and 'borrowed' them. It looked horribly like another disaster.

One from Winch and the Giant Groundsel

It was the comforting smell of woodsmoke that hauled me up the final few hundred metres of slippery trail. Mandara was close, and I thought I caught a freckle of light up there above the trees. Or was it a star? Pete, Maggie and Kate were waiting in the dry.

'Where are Dick and Michèle?'

'Just behind. Not far. Any tea going? Pete, where are the bikes?'

'Down the hill, where we left them this morning. Tell you all about it in a minute.'

(Dick) We arrived at Mandara a few minutes after Simon. We had moved quickly the whole way up, stopping just a couple of times to rest our legs and ease our aching shoulders from the rucksack straps. Our clothes were wet through and sticking to our bodies. The path had turned very muddy. In places a stream ran down the trail scooping out potholes and washing down branches. The close heat of the morning had changed to a severe chill and we arrived shivering and eager to hunt out warm clothes and our dry thermal layers.

As we came into the centre of the camp we looked for our party. The obvious clues, the bikes, were difficult to spot. Kate keapt out from behind a pile of rucksacks and waved 'Over here'. Hot tea was high on our list of priorities and Maggie was brewing up. Michèle and I had not found the bikes down the hill at the agreed spot so it was obvious that Pete had lugged them up here and parked them discreetly out of sight. After all, a couple of mountainbikes 10,000 ft up an African mountain can cause a bit of a stir.

'Mandara' turned out to be the location name for a whole collection of neat steep-roofed Scandinavian chalets provided by the Norwegian Aid Agency. Each chalet sleeps six to eight people in comfort and there is a large communal two-storey chalet which is used as the eating house. Most trekkers on organised expeditions have food cooked by porters, and sleep in their own small private chalets. We seemed to be the only people camping out in tents.

After a mug of tea I tackled Pete about a subject that was vexing me to distraction.

'So, what's happened to the bikes?'

'Left them in the bushes, well hidden, near where we stopped this morning. They're safe. Don't worry.'

The subject was dropped for the time being, while dollops of spaghetti bolognese were spooned onto plates. We sat around the hissing petrol stove gabbling our stories of the day, comparing notes and all wanting to be the one who got the wettest, coldest and most desperate. We all had wet clothes, but more seriously a couple of the sleeping bags, and one of the high-altitude down jackets, had also become waterlogged; somehow we'd need to dry them before we reached the higher, colder parts of the mountain.

The topic of drying out became one of hot (or rather, moist) debate. Without access to home-comforts such as radiators, log fires and tumble dryers, the business of making sodden clothing wearable presented a major challenge. I favoured the system of sandwiching a wet garment between two dry ones, wearing it for a few hours and letting body heat do the drying. It was an effective solution, especially if you slept in the wet garment too, but it had the slight disadvantage that you spent many hours feeling cold and clammy. Pete was a great advocate of the 'hold it in front of the petrol-stove for a few minutes' camp. It's a practice that fills the entire area with sock-steam, so is fairly anti-social, and on more than one occasion it resulted in the spontaneous combustion of the sock leaving little more than a singed circle of carbonised poly-cotton in the owner's fingers. Maggie pioneered the dubious practice of tying wet gloves around hot billy-cans of food, and this worked fine so long as everyone remembered they were there; in the semi darkness it was easy to spill food, and there's nothing worse than pulling on a glove and finding the fingers are full of cold semolina. A variation on my body-drying was an idea borrowed from Ados, which he used on the Himalayan run. Young Adrian would put on wet clothes underneath a Goretex suit then embark on violent physical activity which would create a cauldron of steam inside the Goretex. Like the one-way valves of pressure cookers, the millions of microscopic pores of the Goretex would allow the steam to escape without letting any cold air in. Dick's drying method was simply to stuff all his wet clothing under a tent flysheet for the night, then in the morning zoom straight out of his sleeping bag into a full suit of sodden gear and move very fast for a couple of hours till everything was dry.

(Dick's diary, 27 December 1984. 21.15 hrs Mandara Hut.) Grub finished. More mugs of tea being brewed. Great way to celebrate my birthday. Forgotten how old I am. Must be at least 21 or 22. Big Sis cooked birthday cake. Michèle has carried it hidden all the way here for surprise. Fascinating mixture of chewy coconut and sticky flour. All delicately coloured by Bar's children JJ and Adrian. Big dollops of blue and green. Memorable.

Maggie and Michèle are official tea monitors. Pete is engrossed in stacks of food, plastic bags, tins, soggy boxes and a kilo of peanuts which has split open. He's trying

---

Opposite: The National Park is particularly concerned about environmental damage to more sensitive areas of Kilimanjaro such as the Saddle, where every footstep away from the trail can leave scars which last for years.

to bring some order to our chaotic catering. Kate is studying coat buttons with a bearded
German trekker. Nick is busy with his wet underpants trying to sandwich them between
a towel over his head and a balaclava to hold them in place. Ados will be fascinated: he
never dreamt up this use for a Helly Hansen. Sometimes Nick gets really fanatical about
the minutiae of life. Luckily only Pete knows where the bikes are, otherwise Nick would
have them on the table, and I would have to feign enthusiasm and clean my chain or
check my headset for tomorrow. No point in checking 'cos we'll find pretty soon if
anything's gone wrong. In my experience, mechanical things are best left alone: too
much readjustment simply puts them further out of equilibrium.

At Mandara the tents were pitched on one of the few available patches of level
ground. It was midnight when we turned in. It had stopped raining and as we stood
listening to the dripping of leaves the sky began to split and the heavy clouds slipped
aside to let a few stars wink a goodnight.

Slippin' an' Slidin'

I was awoken by the chatter of departing porters. Rivers of dew were running down
the walls of the tent, and when a finger was pushed against the fabric, the water
would hurry down even faster. We'd overslept; not surprising after the minimal
quotas of shut-eye we'd been having recently.

The long grass around the tents was sparkling in the bright warm sun, tingly and
fresh to walk through with bare feet. Breakfast was a bright orange plastic bowl full
of muesli and mango, washed down with mugs of tea. We were all excited: there's a
wonderful anticipant thrill to waking up on the slopes of a mountain, knowing you're
going higher. And higher. And that for several days life is going to be uniquely simple,
with just the one goal of reaching the top. Every foot climbed increases the
commitment and distances you further and further from the maelstrom of mundane
activities with which we seem able to fill our existence.

We had done well so far. All the gear was on the mountain, with the notable
exception of the chocolate, which had been left by mistake in a fridge in Nairobi. This
was actually a bit serious, since we'd planned to use it as a major part of our diet at
high altitude. With the disappearance of our sugar also, we were very low on 'instant
energy' foods. But the bikes were going well, and everyone was fit. If all went
according to plan, we'd be camping at the Horombo Hut by nightfall, then continue
to Kibo Hut the next day. From there we'd see what the weather and terrain looked
like before making our summit push.

As the tents were being shaken and folded, Dick became embroiled in convoluted
negotiations with the porters.

(Dick. Mandara Hut morning start.) 'Nicas. How many porters have we got?'
'Eight, Mr Crane, Sir,' he replied.
'But we've eight packs here and only seven men have picked them up. Where's the
eighth man? Or are you a porter too?'
'No. I'm a guide. Guides don't carry loads. We have work to do.' Nicas is pretty
clever. He's our guide. He realises that in our western society working intellectuals don't
have to do manual labour. When with Romans do as the Romans do. He wore a smart

black 'Manhattan Yacht Club' T shirt and sported a bright blue 'Yankee Dodgers' cap.

'Nicas. Where's the other porter?'

'They're all here,' he replied calmly, his pearly white teeth flashing with an innocent smile.

'But I see only seven.'

'That's right. The other man is carrying food for me. Each guide has his own porter.'

'But we hired eight men. Who carried the extra pack yesterday?' Nicas casually pointed out that both Nick and I had lugged a big rucksack up the mountain. I started to panic when I realised that we might be left with all the extra gear to carry. Frantic reshuffling of loads was out of the question because each of the seven had selected the pack they wanted and tied their possessions on board. Only the largest pack remained. The silent seven looked amused. Nicas looked clever. We, no doubt, looked stupid, and felt it, so I said,

'What can we do, Nicas?'

He replied, 'Maybe hire another porter, maybe these porters can help, but I think that the load is too heavy. A suitable fee can be arranged.'

Ah ha! the situation became clear: finance might win the day. A little discussion persuaded a couple of porters to club together and share the load. One set off with a double rucksack, the other with a sack on his head and a petrol can in his hand.

Once the porters had departed, Dick, Pete and I picked up our packs and headed back downhill to collect the bikes from their hiding place. We ran down in the sunshine, taking twenty minutes to reach the clearing. Pete led us across the grass hummocks and down the slope to the stunted bushes that we'd sprawled among while writing *The Sunday Times* report the day before. He rooted around in the undergrowth, mumbled 'That's funny', stood up, moved sideways a bit and started pulling at the bushes. I was slightly baffled, because Pete was looking for the bikes in exactly the spot that I'd searched meticulously yet unsuccessfully the night before. Dick shouted: 'Can you see them, Pete?' I was just starting to feel uneasy, when Pete fought his way back through the scrub shouting 'They've gone, the bikes have gone!'

After several seconds of cataplectic seizure I was overwhelmed by the parallel urges to heap vile abuse upon Pete for not hiding the bikes well enough the night before, and to be violently sick. I was still deciding which to do first when Dick asked where exactly Pete had left them.

'I quite definitely buried them right here, under a load of branches'. He pointed to a heap of scrub. 'But they've gone. They were both just here (pointing again), side by side. Somebody must have found them and ridden them off down the hill. They are quite marketable after all.' I just couldn't believe how Pete could be so casual about an event that had effectively dealt a death-blow to the whole expedition.

'Maybe you've forgotten where you put them,' I said hopefully, and began attacking the undergrowth like a ferret in a frenzy. 'They must be here *somewhere*.'

'Tell you what,' Pete began, 'since we haven't got all day to mess around, let's be logical about this. I left the bikes right here where I'm standing. And since I hid them so well, it's impossible that anyone could have found them. Therefore they must still be here, under my feet.' I looked at him, smelling a rat.

'You bilge-licker, you absolute festering b...'

Above: The closer we rode to Kibo Summit, the more impossible looked the final climb. Uhuru Peak itself is hidden by high clouds.

Below: Despite the sun, the air temperature hovered around zero, and with the added wind-chill factor our thermal Berghaus jackets were essential.

Above: Mawenzi, at 16,890 feet, provided a dramatic backdrop during the first part of our ride across the Saddle towards the main peak of Kilimanjaro.

Below: On our third day we found ourselves racing against the weather as clouds started to close in around us.

'In fact, here they are! Look, silly me's been standing on them all the time!'

Pete rolled back into paroxysms of hysterical laughter while Dick and I tugged our beloved machines out from under a cunningly constructed mat of dense foliage. No wonder we hadn't found them the night before; they were completely invisible. I was weak with relief. The score was one trick each.

We raced back up to Mandara, stamping the pedals and bouncing the bikes in and out of the deep muddy gullies that snaked through the bushes. A brief pause at the Hut's water trough to top up our two bottles, and then into the jungle. We didn't get far. There are two ways of getting from Mandara to Horombo, a steep and precipitous mud ladder that squirms shoulder-wide through dense forest, and a longer, gentler more open route that is ideal for riding mountainbikes. You can imagine which we ended up on.

Only a few hundred yards beyond the Hut, and we were off the bikes, lifting them over prostrate tree trunks four foot high. And it got better: roots, poking from the earth like half-buried limbs sidetracked our tyres sending us outstretched onto cushions of jungle shrubbery. In places the muddy path narrowed to a few inches, with long steep drops to one side, and there were a couple of scrambles, where the bike had to be shouldered and humped up while hands and feet dug in the mud. It was dirty, sweaty, hard work and fun.

The path was seldom straight for more than a few feet at a time, climbing and winding towards 10,000 feet. Sunlight filtered through the canopy above, playing on the lush array of deep greens like dappled shadows on a sea-floor. One of many excursions into the rough brought me nose-to-petal with *Impatiens Kilimanjari*, a tiny flower with a livid red gaping snapdragon mouth and curly yellow tail. In the all-enveloping viridescence of burgeoning jungle, these bright spots of colour caught the eye like lights in the night.

Despite having to carry the bikes, we were moving slightly faster than the few trekkers who were out in the jungle that day, so during the course of the morning we overtook several parties. Many would try and make it as far as Horombo Hut at the top of the jungle, then return to the bottom; a few would press on to Kibo and beyond. They were always fun to talk to, and I suspect that we provided breaks of light entertainment that relieved their toils.

(Dick) 'Yes. You are real. I have read about you in ze newspaper in Austria. Now I can see you. And still I do not believe.'

The Austrian was a really nice chap, with a weathered face and fast, neat eyes, about fifty, well-educated and looking comfortably stout in his white safari suit and cream bush hat. He thought we were 'madmen on wheels', and leant over to examine us as if through a monocle. We told him all about I.T. and our special bicycles, and he made hasty jottings in a field note-book.

If he thought we looked pretty odd, then it's fair to say that he was not exactly normal either. Nick and I were ideally equipped for mountain-climbing, in our expedition salopettes, Brasher boots and survival rucksacks. The laundered Austrian was shod in walking shoes at 10,000 feet above the clouds, in a steamy jungle, in darkest Africa. He was accompanied by his wife who was wearing a mid-length white skirt, and a porter bearing a huge black tin trunk on his head. We smiled while the lady took a photograph.

We had to stop several times on the tight jungle path to let through trekkers and porters heading down to Mandara. Time and again we explained that we were hoping to ride our bicycles high on the mountain; time and again we were countered with shaking heads.

Free from having to organise, and flitting through the forest with just a pack-full of emergency gear, I felt happy. As a mountainbike route, the jungle trail was a technical pleasure palace. On most of that tortuous track it would have been quicker to carry the bike, but the challenge was too tempting to ignore, and even the chance of riding the bike for five feet was worth the effort of setting it down, leaping on and 'going for it'. I was sad when we unexpectedly rode out of our cosy verdant tree-world and into a bright sunny heath-land.

(Dick) It was like an alpine meadow, dotted with flowers. Suddenly we found we could unshoulder the bikes and ride long stretches. Hard-packed earth made an excellent surface to cycle over. It was undulating; not too steep and with no sudden steps. We found it possible to use the gears here, changing up for long level straights of ten or more yards, and then back down for steep sections, or tussocky grass.

We reached a junction in the track, and used it as an excuse to pull out our map and flop onto the grass for a breather. The landscape had opened out. Above our shoulders stood the serrated spires of Mawenzi, the smaller of Kilimanjaro's twin peaks, and there in the far distance, rising into the clouds, we could see the rounded bulk of Kibo itself. It looked a very long way off. After some easy riding, we found ourselves contouring round the side of the mountain on a desperately rough track which climbed in and out of narrow gullies filled with tumbling streams.

(Dick) Gully-riding is a special technique. Going down, you hang your bottom out over the back wheel to prevent the bike going head over heels, rear brake on fairly firm; front brake only used slightly. All the jolting and jarring of the descent as the bike jockeys down rocks is taken on the forearms and knees. They act as human shock-absorbers, keeping your body at a roughly constant height above the ground while the bike bucks and twists over the irregular pits and boulders.

Across the stream at the bottom, with a great splash, then up the other side of the gully we flick into lower gears and quickly slowed to ultra-low ratio. With our Bike UK gear modification, one turn of the pedals equalled a seven-eighths turn of the rear wheel; so slow that it was often difficult to keep the bike balanced upright. It's slower than walking pace. We called this gear 'winch', and found it excellent on open, steep slopes where the surface allowed good tyre traction. On anything even slightly slippery, the terrific torque this ultra-low gear produced would spin the rear wheel and have us off.

We both agreed that our favourite uphill gear of all was the second to lowest (26 inches). We dubbed it 'one from winch' and used it for most of our climbing. It gives the strength to tackle a hill combined with sufficient speed for easy balance and a pedal rev rate which is not manic. If Nick disappeared around a corner ahead, I would yell out, 'What next?', and often the answer would come back as a happy shout of 'One from winch'.

There are two techniques for climbing depending on the slope to be tackled. On long slopes we found the steady controlled approach to be the best, with the bike set in low

Left: Gilman's Point (top dead centre) on the crater rim, at 18,000 feet, is reached by a 3,000-foot scree of rhomb porphyry lava rising above Kibo Hut.

Above: Michèle at our Kibo camp, preparing one of the many cans of tea we drank to counter high-altitude dehydration.

Below: Sorting gear at Kibo camp, ready for the final assault.

gear before the climb started. The important factor is to ensure that the tyres have enough traction. The rear wheel needs sufficient load to hold the ground and the front wheel must be held down firm enough for steerage. The distribution of bodyweight is crucial. It is better to remain seated for as long as possible because the movement is smoother. However you need to bend double over the handlebars as the slope gets steeper until you must stand and lean forward staring at your knobbly front tyre inching up the slope. Jerky movements must be avoided, because once a wheel has slipped it's well nigh impossible to find your rhythm again.

The other type of slope we became more than familiar with was the short, sharp 1 or 2-foot vertical step and 4 to 5-foot steep bank. These obstacles are the territory of true mountainbike fans, and technique must be accompanied by a surge of high spirits and confidence. I hit vertical steps hard and heartily. A good turn of speed is useful. As you approach the step, say half a wheel-diameter away, get physical with the handlebars and give them a great skyward hoist. This lifts the rubber of the front tyre onto the lip of the step, at which point you put some power into the back wheel. Make sure that your bottom is clear of the seat and your weight is well forward, with your legs ready to flex as the bike rides up.

The 4 to 5-foot banks could for me be the most frustrating challenges. By definition these are the slopes that are too steep or have too little traction to ride up in 'controlled winch mode'. In general they will be higher than a wheel diameter, and thus too high to jump, but no higher than a tall man. Brute force wins the day here, with a little help from a high gear, say 3rd or 4th from bottom, and an even weight distribution between wheels. Start building up speed well back from the slope so that you're stabilised before you hit the action. Try to pedal smoothly and continuously all the time, maintaining breakneck speed. If it works, then it's all over in a flash; if it doesn't work, then you'll know it!

With time and practice, you become more and more in control of the machine. These frantic amateur methods are replaced by the cool, considered approach of the professional who can mount a three-foot log without a scream or descend a near-vertical six-foot drop with no more than a wry smile. Mountainbike experts Geoff Apps and Chris Simmons tell us that control is all important.

As in any problem solving, there's no substitute for pre-selection of a good line. For most of the route up Kilimanjaro, we had no time to walk the ground before we rode. The intricacies of route choice around rocks, down potholes, over loose gravel or muddy banks, had to be resolved as we reached each obstacle. In general, loose gravel and cobbles were best avoided. Boulders, rocks and tussocks of grass up to one foot high were generally no problem if they were firmly fixed to the ground and taken confidently, at speed. Loose cobbles from 3 to 6 inches in diameter were terminal; the only chance with these is to hit the tops of them at Mach 2 or 3, flying just above the ground, hoping that sheer enthusiasm supports you. If the cobbles last for more than six feet, then enthusiasm is not enough.

Tree roots, branches and shiny tips of boulders were all potential hazards. These may be only a few inches high, but can be slippery as ice. However chunky your tyres, there is zero to negative traction on these devils, and your wheels can take unpredictable lateral excursions, leaving you sprawling in the bushes. Our principle was to avoid them, but where there was no option, attack them front on, aiming straight at the centre, at right angles to the surface of danger.

The mountainbike rule was: if it's solid and firm, attack it; if it's loose or slippery, avoid it.

The secret of cross-country cycling lies with the micro-terrain, not the overall landscape. High mountain ridges, like those of Skiddaw, Helvellyn or the Red Cuillins, can be ridden because the micro-terrain is finely-ground hard-packed gravel. Subdued hills and valleys like the Brecon Beacons or the seafront at Brighton can be virtually impossible because of their looseness and dissected nature.

In these early miles, before the altitude began to take effect, there was a fair amount of competition between the two of us. Most of the time, the track was only wide enough for one bike, so we'd take it in turns to be out in the front blazing the trail. Going uphill, it was always easier to ride behind: if I saw Dick's wheels slip from under him on a certain section of track, I'd always got a few seconds' grace to pick an alternative route and see if I could get higher than he before keeling over myself. It was a matter of honour to be the one who managed to ride furthest up a slope before admitting defeat.

(Dick) Each tumble was an excuse for a long discussion on the previous section. A continuous thirty-yard ride might take nearly ten minutes to describe in detail to each other: how we rounded left of that boulder, jumped over the loose stones, slipped on the tussock but held our line through the groove. The altitude and thin air were already becoming apparent, and these halts were opportunities for heavy gasping and an attempt to stabilise our heart-rates. Hearty laughter added to the gay banter, and the warm African sun made for an altogether enjoyable experience.

Late for a Date

With the height, came the cold and cloud. The T-shirts we'd been wearing through the jungle were no longer enough to keep us warm, and out on the exposed flanks of Mawenzi, with wraiths of chilly mist chasing us upwards, we had to burrow in our packs for thermal vests. These long-sleeved garments were ideal for biking, being tight-fitting and stretchy, with no openings for the cold to get in. The terrain was getting harder too, and increasingly we had to carry the bikes up gullies and across stretches of outsize boulders.

'Bit of a shame about the rad-pads', Dick commented after settling the hard metal tubing of his mountainbike across his shoulders for the umpteenth time that day. It was indeed. When we'd tackled the '14 Peaks' in Wales all those months ago, our bikes had been fitted with wrap-around foam pads on the down-tubes of the frames, which took some of the pain out of shouldering the machine. But this time the pads had been forgotten, and now we were really paying for it. Each time we put our feet down, the shock-loading on our shoulders compressed the existing bruises. We'd have to find a way of padding the bike frames or end up with permanent troughs across our shoulders.

Continually getting on and off the bikes had slowed us down. We had planned to meet Kate, Maggie and Michèle for lunch, agreeing that they should wait for us in a sheltered spot. With the track coursing round and up, we could seldom see more than

Above: On the lower part of Kibo's scree, riding was possible but difficult in the thin air.
Below: We stop to catch our breath on the day-long slog with Nicas and Pete up the scree to Gilman's Point.
Right: Climbing to 18,000 feet.

fifty yards ahead, so had no idea where they had got to. When finally we came upon our team it was mid-afternoon.

We flew down the very Scottish hillside whooping with accomplishment and demonstrating our superlative mountainbiking skills with an all-action live display of sliding and jumping, balance and daring, then tangled pedals and fell in the stream, to a derisive accompaniment of 'Pathetic' and 'Wimps'.

(Dick's diary.) Lunch was shared dates, cashew nuts and left-over coconut birthday cake. We lay in a shallow scoop, out of the wind, beside a stream and soaked up the sun. A rough woody plant like Scottish heather cushioned our sprawl, and golden tussocks of grass added colour. Patches of bare dust and gravel were appearing between clustered plants. The limits of vegetation were obviously close above. Dainty little blue flowers, bell-like, several to a stem, sheltered under the heather. A few sparse wiry bushes four-foot high were scattered around.

The strangest plants, like freak triffids marching down the slopes, are the giant groundsel. They have thick chunky stems like an elephant's thigh, and are topped by a crown of spiky green leaves. They are most peculiar, up to ten foot high and hard as oak. Nick climbed up into one and looked quite at home.

The rest of Day 2 was spent in cloud as we laboured up towards Horombo Hut, 'laboured' because the chilly damp air, thinning oxygen and complicated riding all added up to a fair degree of effort. Wherever the path levelled, and we escaped from the boulder-fields, we'd find ourselves trying to pedal through sections of marsh that threatened to suck the tyres down, or through mazes of high grass tussocks separated by narrow wet alleys that always seemed to catch the pedals as we tried to squeeze through. On the few lengths of hard surface, it was tempting to turn on the speed; it was at the end of these that we had a major up-ending.

We were racing along in line astern, my front wheel just a couple of inches behind Dick's bike. Without warning my cousin just disappeared from view. Instinct made me pull for the brakes, but it was too late to slow the bike and the Saracen nose-dived over the edge into the bog below. I saw the rocks coming, and managed a half forward roll, cushioning the collision with my hand, then forearm and shoulder before being flicked onto my back by the momentum. My head was about the only part that didn't hit rock. I came to a halt a few feet from Dick. We lay there a while, feeling quite beaten up; doing an anatomical damage-control. No broken bones, and fortunately, the bikes were completely unhurt. It was lucky they'd landed on the soft, marshy ground, rather than the rocks which could well have bent the forks.

(Dick's diary, 28 December 1984. 22.00 hrs. Horombo Hut.) Unfortunate accident 1,000 ft below here. Me in lead. Saw steep step. Whipped hard left, brakes on. Stopped OK but stood on bendy heather and keeled over. Nick must be blind. He powered on straight over the drop. Did a rather grand concertina with his face and legs. Very lucky to miss some rocks. Felt sorry for him, so feigned injury. That made him feel better. Good excuse to lie and rest.

Twelve thousand feet was a psychological threshold: the level at which most people begin to be affected by the lack of oxygen in the air. We crossed the imaginary altitude-suffering line an hour or so before reaching Horombo, marking the occasion by a session of communal wingeing about breathlessness. We must have looked quite a sight: Dick's face was smeared with mud, pale and thin-looking beneath a mat of damp hair. His forearms were filthy with slime from bogs and his once-white I.T. shirt was splattered in peat-stains which had flicked off the front wheel. Both of us had wet feet from fording streams, and were muddy up to knee level.

We were standing propped on the bikes deep in post-tumble conversation when three mountain guides jogged out of the mist above us, pushing along the only other wheeled-vehicle on Kilimanjaro. About six foot long and three wide, it's a flat wooden platform crossed by a couple of straps, on top of a single large wheel. There are two handles at each end, and at full-throttle this human-powered machine can top eight miles per hour. With a man at front and back it has excellent manoeuvrability and good acceleration. When the pneumatic tyre hits a rock, the thing leaves the ground completely, and the scars along its superstructure told of past collisions with immovable, most likely granitic, objects.

This is the Kilimanjaro ambulance, used for rescuing the injured and incapacitated from the mountain, and if ever there was a strong motive for not hurting yourself, it was the prospect of a ride on this mono-wheeled hybrid.

Our last mile of the day was suitably sedate.

Cycling the permanent snows of the crater rim could be fast but risky as we tried to balance in the frozen ruts.

Horombo

Our arrival at Horombo created a stir of interest among the incumbent residents. From open doors surprised faces watched a couple of pedal bicycles being ridden across the grit patch in front of the huts, 12,500 feet above sea-level, way above the clouds. They then saw the bicycles leant againt a wooden post, and one of the riders lurch up some step crying 'Where are the tea-bags!'.

But 'putting on a brew' was not be a straightforward operation. For while the six of us had arrived at Horombo within a few minutes of each other, our various rucksacks were nowhere to be seen. Simon had been spotted a couple of hours back along the trail, carrying what Michèle guessed was the pack containing the tents, but the whereabouts of the other packs was a mystery. Pete and I wandered off to look for a level spot to pitch the tents. There was a slight rise behind the huts, and even walking up this made me breathless; we'd arrived not only at Horombo, but at the threshold of oxygen debt.

It was at Horombo that we enjoyed our 'Last Great Feast.' When finally the rest of our gear arrived, Pete and Dick gallantly disappeared to put up the tents, while many feverish hands rooted in rucksacks for the food. Around a long wooden table in the communal hut, an exquisite repast was concocted. By the light of a single candle, we waded through an enormous goat meat stew, carried from Nairobi in a plastic carrier bag. To bulk it out we cooked a cauldron of pasta. Michèle then had a masterful vision. Using some flour that had turned up in the rucksacks full of bike spares, she stirred up a concoction that when cooked closely resembled chapatis; with the stew, they were delicious. Surrounded by the darkness of the hut, the six of us sat by our guttering candle, nibbling at extra chapatis spread with jam and sipping scalding coffee.

The petrol stoves took some getting used to, and to get them to perform at their best, the operator had to stick to a set procedure: top up the tank with juice; pump up a small amount of pressure; light the flame and release a lever simultaneously, then pump up the pressure to operating level. The natural 'fire-maker' in the team was Pete, who's been known to create rustic blast-furnaces that can bring a cooking-pot to red-heat. I treated the petrol stoves with some trepidation at first, having once caused a Primus stove to burst into flames and grow so hot that all the soldered joints melted and it fell into its separate constituent parts. It's a trait that I inherited from

Kibo peak from the Horombo camp

Hol, for he once managed to burn the front of his tent off while camping in the Lake District. We had no bad incidents with our trusty Coleman stoves, and even I managed to learn how to work them after a couple of days.

(Dick's diary.) I rose at dawn. The sun cut in low and cool from the east. The sky was pale and the plains of Tanzania could be seen through the mist thousands of feet below. The glittering circle on the right is the town of Moshi, with lights still burning at 6 am. Tent zips were still firmly fastened in our encampment. Nearby cheery trekkers were up and out of their huts, busily washing themselves and packing bags ready for another day's adventure. I had a pee and went back to bed. Two hours later Nick dragged out our Peak 1 petrol stove and got some tea on the boil.

(Dick) We had a full team talk. We had finished the fun; we had got ourselves with bikes onto the mountain; and we had the porters and equipment roughly organised if cumbersome. Ahead lay adventure. As they say in the movies 'Stepping into the unknown.'

Michèle, Nick, Pete and myself all knew basic mountain craft. We needed to check that Maggie and Kate carried survival gear and knew how to use it. Each person with spare warm top garment, Goretex water/wind proof outer shell (for Nick, Pete and I our Berghaus jackets fulfilled both requirements, whilst Michèle had what I consider to be a piece of ancient history: the very same Troll/Goretex jacket which had been right along the length of the Himalayas), spare food, water bottle, compass, torch, balaclava, gloves, snow/sun goggles and UV cream. We had all started our Diamox tablets for altitude sickness and were ready to descend to lower altitudes if symptoms got bad.

As important as having these items is the knowledge of how to use them. We made it clear that as one cools down due to rain, snow, wind or tiredness, then it is vital to conserve body heat and seal it in before too late: tighten drawstrings, use scarf or balaclava, don't ever say 'I'm too cold to bother putting on my spare clothes and anyway I'll make it to the tents.'

I felt reassured to have got this far. The bikes were in fine fettle, and everyone was feeling well. This journey was ready to metamorphose into a real adventure. I remembered my climb of Cotopaxi six years ago and how the simple ascent had become a serious struggle up the ice. I knew that Nick was good enough to get himself, even laden down with bike, to the summit. It might become slow and difficult but he could do it. Equally, Pete would not be a burden on us. His extensive mountain experience covered all the standard routes and theory and more besides.

The girls caused me slight worry. Kate and Maggie were both 'unknown quantities' to me. Maggie had the air of an inquisitive tourist when I first met her but I have seen her at work over the past few days and she finds herself fully at home here, and clearly no newcomer to backpacking. She expressed on the approach march a healthy fear and respect for the upper slopes of Kilimanjaro, and that should stand her in good stead. To appreciate a problem is half way to solving it.

I was fretting: we had a long day in front of us if we were to reach Kibo hut by dark, yet before we could leave, the bikes needed checking over and we had to fashion some carrying pads for them. And we'd have to endure the now customary two hours of haggling with the porters. Unless we all moved quickly, we'd end up stuck at Horombo till midday. It seemed ages before the others were out of their sleeping bags and into 'active mode.'

Dick was still frustrated by the play in his headset; to a casual listener, his early morning mutterings about 'having to fix some loose balls in my head' must have sounded like a self-diagnosis of an obscure psychiatric disorder. Since he set about rectifying his malady clad in long-johns, a string vest, yellow sunglasses and a French beret pulled down over his ears, his attire was well-suited to the apparent complaint. In fact Dick's incurable fascination with the precise adjustment of his headset had begun during the Rift Valley work-out, re-ignited in the early hours of the morning before leaving Marangu Gate, then been kindled periodically whenever there'd been a vacuum in the conversation into which he could slot comments like 'Headset's playing up' or 'Must be the play in this bike's steering that's making me fall off.' Horombo was to be the point at which cousin Richard was determined to fix his bike once and for all.

Close inspection revealed that there was nothing on either bike that had been damaged . . . yet. Pete and I adjusted all the wheel bearings now that they'd had a chance to bed in, and looked carefully over the frames for cracks and bends in the tubing. The tyres were still at the pressures we'd started with, and amazingly didn't show any signs of wear. I was conscious that this would be a last chance to satisfy myself that the bicycles were 100%, because once we got stuck into the higher altitudes there simply wouldn't be the brain-power and energy to accomplish maintenance chores. Showing unusual foresight, I even checked the brakes, adjusting them precisely so that they'd be ready when needed in three or four days, for the big downhill.

(Dick's diary, 29 December 1984, 09.30 hrs. Horombo Hut, on rock with cup of tea.) Goddamit, I'm frustrated today. Three and a half hours daylight gone and we're still messing around. I finished my ball race hours ago. Now I'm twiddling my thumbs waiting for the rest to catch up. Come on, you slobs.

Nick and Pete are bent double over the rear end of a bike. Spanners and screwdrivers and deep discussion. They're probably rebuilding the hub so that Nick can clip onto a rope and jumar himself up the volcano. Michèle is pumping like mad on a petrol stove whilst Maggie holds a cigarette lighter underneath and they try to see if they can blow themselves up. Kate has interrogated me ten times saying, 'Porridge. Where's the porridge oats?'. Now she's completely reverse packing two rucksacks into each other.

Here comes Nicas to pester us about stuffing our packs and moving on. Stuff him. We're not ready yet.

What a waste of time it is having a support crew. I spend all my time organising them. If you want so much as a pinch of salt you have to unpack at least six rucksacks. Even then all you find is half a million plastic bags of unlabelled white powder. It could be mashed potato, milk, flour, sugar or salt for all I know. Each night all the junk has to be spread out over the ground so that we can try to piece together enough equipment to put up a tent or boil a mug of tea. Gone are the free-and-easy days of two-man travel with no more than the bare essentials, when we carried so little that we could find anything in half a second in the dark. Big expeditions are a joke. No wonder so many take so long to do not very much.

Nick's a pain in the arse. He's so bloody efficient; up first, makes jolly cups of tea, plans today's route, busily takes down tent, now he's readjusting bike to make it super-duper fast. In my mind's eye, I can see him already out on the climb; with a gleam in his eye, sinewy muscles standing out like flick knives, furrowed brow in concentration, straining at the pedals. I'll be floundering along again, looking at the dirt flying off his rear wheel and getting gravel flicked in my face.

We were discussing the frame-padding issue when the dreaded porter confrontation re-ignited. Nicas decided he could wait no longer for us, and came over to ask when our big rucksacks would be packed and ready to carry. Suddenly there was mayhem as porters arrived and started picking up half-full packs.

Frantically trying to keep an eye on all the packs, all six of us gathered for an impromptu conference. We seemed to be carrying far more than necessary, and the logic was to leave a cache of surplus equipment at Horombo. Lighter loads would ease the porter problem. Anything that wasn't vital for reaching the summit was to be jettisoned. Ruthlessly, everyone sorted their personal gear and made growing piles of clothing, books, bottles and bits and pieces that definitely wouldn't be needed for the climb. Then, when nobody was looking we each put half of our piles back in our summit sacs, and, in a show of exaggerated magnamity, carried our 'surplus gear' to the pack that was to be left at Horombo. In this way, we lightened our communal load by many ounces: the sacrificial bag ended up containing a bar of soap, a pair of boots, one sock and a printed frock.

Since Dick and I were personally going to have to carry the bike tools and spares, and since these were mostly made of metal and therefore heavy, the two of us applied more discerning eyes over the heavy-metal pile than we did over our personal clothing collections. After due consideration, we decided to dump the wrench we'd brought for removing freewheels, together with the molegrips and the specialist tools like the block removers and bottom-bracket spanners, and spare parts such as a rear derailleur, two tyres, and a freewheel. We reasoned that since the bikes were now 'broken in', they would need no more adjustments for the time being, and that all we needed for our summit riding were the tools necessary to mend punctures and, say, convert the gearing from 15 speeds to one speed in the event of derailleurs being smashed. If there was a major accident to one of the bikes, we'd simply have to pick up the bits and carry them.

After our radical re-think of what constituted a 'necessary tool or spare' all we had left in our pile for the summit was one inner tube, one tyre, a puncture repair kit, a chain-splitting tool, screwdriver, spanners for the brakes and a set of Allen keys. The bike spares and tools we were leaving filled an entire kit-bag; it grieved me that all this weighty hardware had been carried so far up the mountain, and was now destined never to be used. The bikes were proving too reliable by half.

Dick's diary (Horombo Hut, 29 December 1984, 10.30 hrs. Sitting on rock without cup of tea.) Got rid of all the porters now. Time for a rest. Everything has been reshuffled and excess equipment left behind. Nicas wanted to help us sort it out. I would like to let him join in more but it is awkward because we are different from the normal trekkers' expedition. The porters have waited a long time and they're obviously keen to be on the move. They tell me that late afternoon typically brings rain and mist, they want the shelter at Kibo Hut before then.

We've had the battle of loads again; the porters stand around the packing-up and when a pack is released for a moment they grab it and pretend that it is their pack for the day. I can't blame them because we in our turn are running around busily stuffing as much extra gear as we can into their packs to save ourselves weight.

Solomon; he's the shifty one, always hanging around close by, wears a shabby grey raincoat, is a bit thin in the face and bows his shoulders. Whilst all the others were waiting around the tents and cooking gear to get the best packs, he stood across to one side behind Nick and Pete. I couldn't work out why. Now it's obvious: he's got the pack with the spare tyre tied to the back. The most prestigious pack on the mountain. He's the only porter who is clearly identified as belonging to 'the crazy English cyclists'. Good for him. I reckon he's a good 'un really, possibly somewhat shy.

Wrong Turning

The porter problem disappeared as suddenly as it had come; once the main rucksacks were packed, they swiftly shouldered them and strode up the slope and out of sight, leaving us peaceful at last, sitting a little forlorn in the centre of a small gritty plateau surrounded by our personal sacs and the bikes. We all relaxed. A sleeping mat had been chosen for the slaughter, and, armed with Pete's penknife Dick and I cut long strips from it and began binding them around the tubing of our bike. We each had our own theories: I put double thickness padding on three of my bike's tubes; Dick put treble thickness on one of his tubes. I used a number of surplus rucksack straps to bind the padding tight; Dick used a mile and a quarter of cotton. The end results looked a little strange, but were equally effective.

The final chore of the morning was to sew I.T. labels onto our clothing, so that we could get the charity noticed in photographs. Because it was cold, and it would have added at least 20 seconds to the task, we kept the clothes on while doing the sewing. Dick, always a meticulous seamster, managed to *appliqué* to the front of his salopettes a large I.T. panel which incorporated a special quick-release system so that he could fold back the panel and release his salopette zip when attending to the needs of nature. I attached the same panel, but managed to sew it not only to the salopettes, but to the T-shirt underneath, and the thermal vest beneath that. I think I also caught up a few loops of skin. The fact that I'd sewn myself in to my garments didn't come to light till a couple of hours later when I paused to irrigate a groundsel. I realised too late, and finished up writhing on the ground, with legs plaited, eyes screwed up and fingers tearing at stitching. I had to be cut free, which saved the day, but not the groundsel.

(Dick's diary.) At 11 am we were on our way. Porters resting for the day at Horombo, gathered to see us off. The first people coming down from Kibo were arriving as we departed. The trail was stony and dry—reminiscent of yesterday— and soon we were back into the old swing of pedal 10 feet; fall off; gasp for breath; lift cycle; plod 20 feet; pedal 10; fall off . . . ad infinitum.

The early people returning from Kibo were soon joined by the first of the haggard-looking but exuberant summiteers of today. These people had risen at midnight at Kibo Hut, climbed the 3,000 feet to Gilman's Point on the crater rim, and then, with ever worsening headaches, done a quick-turn and rushed down to Kibo for a drink, then carried on across the Saddle to Horombo. Hence, by midday, we were meeting people who had already been on the go for twelve gruelling hours. Kibo Hut's at 15,500 feet, and many of them won't have slept a wink there.

After leaving Horombo, we came to a fork in the trail. It wasn't clear which was the main 'prong' and since the cloud covered the slopes and we could see no other humans, we chose at random, the left option. We were full of high spirits, glad to be away from Horombo at long last, and committed now to the hardest part of the climb. We bowled over stones and grit, yelling at each other how great we felt, and wasn't it good to be back on the bikes again. The surface got better and better, and we went faster and faster . . . not surprising since the trail was going downhill. Downhill! Wait a moment. We're meant to be going UP hill.

At that instant a group of slow-moving trekkers materialised out of the mist ahead of us. Their leader, a tall severe man carrying an ebony walking stick, looked as if he knew about things like maps and routes.

'Excuse me, but is this the way to Kibo Hut?' I asked.

'Hello. Wo fahren Sie denn auf diesen Fahrrädern hin?'

'We think we are lost. Where have you come from?'

'Sie sind ja wahnsinnig!'

I turned to Dick (who hasn't the same grasp of German as myself): 'The man says we're on the wrong track. They've come from somewhere called Varnsinig; never heard of the place—they must be more lost than us. Anyway, Kibo Hut can't be downhill from here, so we'd better go back to that other track.'

We turned around and set off back the way we'd come. It was going to be a very, very long Saturday.

Last Water

Dick was so hot under the collar about our taking of the wrong prong that he steamed off up the mountain-side, bike on shoulders, aiming to take a shorter cross-country route back to the correct trail. It was a good move, for we were back on the right track fairly quickly. For a couple of hours we rode fast, hopping off the bikes when we came to a tricky section, rarely speaking, eager to get a few miles under our belts before relaxing. Now and again we'd meet small, dazed-looking groups wandering tiredly back down the mountain.

(Dick) A wide-brimmed green jungle hat leant forwards. Two beady eyes peered out from a parchment-like face. He looked wildly-excited and said 'Are you crazy? Are you going to try to ride those up there?' And he pointed with his stick, at our bikes and back over his shoulder to the slopes of the most beautiful snow peak. The mountain was close enough for us to pick out huge ice-walls on the crest and long black lava ridges down the sides.

'We're going to try.'

'You might be OK for the next few miles onto the Saddle where it is flat and gravelly, but then . . .' his voice trailed off into a whistle.

With sunburnt face and screwed up eyes he really looked bombed out. His clothes were filthy, functional, and a faithful facsimile of a colonial explorer: heavy scuffed hiking boots, pleated pockets and bagginess. There were six others with him. They had obviously enjoyed themselves and I suspected had experienced a rare feeling of achievement on the top. We found throughout our adventure that an unusual bond of friendship links all who venture up to the snows.

'I was sick five times on the way up to the crater,' the man said, as though explaining his madness. I thought: 'That's perseverance.' His friends wanted to know who made our bikes and why we had 'Intermediate Technology' plastered across our chests. It was Nick's turn to give out the spiel, so I took a break and gazed out across the cotton-wool clouds below, then slowly swung round to bring Kibo summit into focus up above. Stupendous. To think that we are here, 4,000 miles away from work, in the middle of Africa on a snowy mountain enjoying ourselves and hopefully doing some good for I.T. I almost needed to pinch myself. It is easy to forget how lucky we are.

The path was levelling out now. Fewer gullies and small ravines to drop down into and climb out of. We were drawing level with the Saddle and some dry brown ash cones were peeking over the col. The wind was getting stronger. An unladen porter came down looking thin and forlorn. He wore only bell-bottom trousers and a red cotton shirt with one button and one safety pin; no socks and shoes several sizes too big.

Presently we came over a steep rocky ridge, rolled down a slope and up to one of Kilimanjaro's best-known landmarks. Standing at the side of a brackish pool which dribbles silently into the surrounding peat, is a single wooden post, at the bottom of which is propped a broken wooden board etched with the ominous words 'Last Water.'

At Horombo people said that there was no water between this shallow puddle and the ice further up the mountain, above Kibo Hut several hours along the trail. We were already thirsty, and slugged two bottles of the cool liquid each before topping up a final time and stowing them in our packs.

(Dick's diary, 29 December 1984, 13.00 hrs.) Soon after midday. Last Water. Turgid pond with green slimy bottom. Drank lots. Filled water bottles with off-grey liquid. Up above fluffy clouds. Blue sky overhead. Crisp air. Pete taking lots of piccies. Nick ridden into a deep wallow in peat bog. Peat up to his ears. He's lying down. Two porters came past. One had no shoes and carried his load on his head. Both big smiles.

Riding passable but not great up to Last Water. Sparse clumped grasses and heather. Dusty soil and fist-sized cobbles. All loose. Fell a lot of times. Terrible traction. Uphill v.diff. Sweating heavily. Air seems real dry, must be altitude. Surely there must be better cycling somewhere? Next time try Karakoram Highway or Mongolian Steppes or Lake Bonneville Salt Flats.

'Last Water' sits in a slight hollow, and on that day it was comfortably out of the wind. We opened our map. To call it a 'map' is being generous. Comprising four sheets of A4 paper glued together, it showed a number of vague pecked lines overlaid on many thin lines which could have been contours, rivers, or both. The photocopier hadn't managed to capture any compass lines, so we had to guess which way was north. Dick traced our route so far, running his finger from Marangu Gate, past Mandara, past Horombo.

'We're somewhere under there' he said definitively stabbing at a lump of peanut butter that had dried onto the map where 'Last Water' should be. 'Just past half-way up Kili as the crow flies, I mean Crane pedals.' The one feature that the map did mark clearly was a broad level-looking plateau at 14,000 feet separating the two peaks of Kibo and Mawenzi. It was marked as 'The Saddle'. We were nearly there.

A Nutty Problem

Dick saw it first, and it provided a good excuse to drop the bikes, stand and stare. To the two of us, starved of smooth fast riding, the Saddle smacked of bikers' paradise. It actually looked flattish. Before us, running up to the base of Kibo, was a broad, brown, dusty desert. Threading across this vastness was a meandering paler buff trail so thin that it merged into the landscape in the middle distance. Kibo itself, the main summit of Kilimanjaro, dominated the view and we could hardly take our eyes from the tantalising spectacle of its snowy summit. It had taken us two-and-a-half days to reach this spot, and it would take the same time again for us to cross this desert, scramble up the formidable-looking slope of Kibo's volcanic cone and make our precarious way around the lip of the summit crater to the true top: Uhuru Peak. Even from where we were standing, four miles away, the angle of Kibo's slopes looked desperately steep for bikes; near the top we could see the cliffs and ice-falls through which we'd have to find a route.

The Saddle was great fun. In places the trail was wide enough to ride side-by-side, but mostly we raced along its gentle surfaces following each other. The tyres raised fine feathers of dust from the bone-dry surface and a fierce sun had our eyes screwed up against the glare. That was what I'd come for: to be riding my bicycle at 14,000 feet along a smooth fast track beneath a blue sky.

(Dick) The Saddle was the only straightforward cycling we had. It reminded me of my childhood cycling. Brother Ados took us out on our first bikes on mountain jaunts. We aimed for the level ridges of Helvellyn back in 1969 and had to carry our drop handlebar racers with specially modified 15 speed gears all the way up. We found thin hard road tyres less than effective at 3,000 feet but at least we had done something which our father had not.

My younger brother Chris was in those days the unassuming stalwart, able to do everything his big brothers could. I was a continual trier and moaner. Ados was the inventor, not just of new jollies but also of mechanical concoctions. He mated a 5-speed derailleur sprocket to a 3-speed Sturmey Archer hub, added a triple chain ring and came up with a 45-speed bike. It worked well and carried him around the Pyrenees one year but weighed a ton.

We three brothers made further attempts to cycle off road, and experimented with straight-lining whereby we picked a compass direction and headed off across heather and hill trying not to deviate.

Chris was the hero who provided Land Rover support, all alone at 18 years old with a couple of plastic bottles of orange juice, on the Lyke Wake Walk. Ados, a friend called Stitch and I cycled the 40 miles in 12¼ hours.

I managed to explore one of the theoretical extremes of using bicycles on mountains when I carried my time trial machine all the way from Langdale in the southern Lakes to Seathwaite in the northern Lakes. All the way over Scafell Pike, England's highest peak, without once putting my foot on the pedals. At the time it struck me as a sensible way of ensuring that I had transport home on the other side, but now I am not so sure.

The girls are having a lot more success up here at 14,000 feet despite total lack of cycling background. Maggie and Kate had bikes when they were small. Michèle, by some lateral thinking better understood by her family than mine, rode a 400 cc Honda motorbike whilst still at school and only got her first pedal cycle when she joined Reading University Pedalling Club at age 19. Strange girl.

From the plains below, and even from the forested lower slopes, you'd have no idea that the Saddle exists. Hidden from sight by the bulging contours of the mountain, it's a secret world; a hinterland between the dense equatorial jungle and the frozen upper slopes. Once on the Saddle, you can no longer see vegetation and the landscape is balanced by the twin peaks of Kibo and Mawenzi, between which the Saddle is suspended. Across this monochrome stage are scattered great rounded boulders, carelessly grouped as if a giant had been playing marbles, got bored and left them lying in the sun. Here and there are long dykes of hard lava, and isolated cones of minor 'parasitic' volcanoes. Our sparkling bicycles and bright blue clothing completed this surreal canvas.

(Dick) As an experiment, we headed off the beaten path, across the open expanses. Once off the hard-packed trail, our wheels sank inches deep into the dry deflation surface of this volcanic plateau. Nigel Winser, of the Expedition Advisory Council, had asked us to beware of damage. There is no soil to bind the dust and pebbles together and our bikes left long, deep scars. With no animals, either large (like rats or mice), or small (like bugs and worms), in the soil, which can turn over the land surface, it may be years before the wind and the action of freeze-thaw manage to erase human prints.

We looked at the grooves with great dismay and headed back to smooth them out with our feet before carrying the bikes to the trail. In some places we could see the boot marks of trekkers who had left the track. Thankfully it seems that most visitors are too tired to go exploring and no doubt the guides are instructed not to encourage wanderers. Mr Nassari of the National Park did seem concerned about conservation of the mountain. I assume that tourism today runs itself and needs no encouragement but his job is to protect the National Park for the future. A small handbook about flora, fauna and geology would be a useful tool to get the message over.

We came upon the three girls sheltering below a low reef of rock while a chill wind hummed overhead. They were freezing, and had been waiting for us for some time. We compared notes on the morning's fun; they'd had a brisk march up from Horombo, enjoying the Saddle as much as we, and had arrived at the lunch-spot a couple of hours ago. They had spent the time nibbling sweets and biscuits between dozes, and were wrapped up tightly against the cold wind. Nicas and Simon had been with them for a while, but the two Tanzanians had departed a while ago, hoping to reach Kibo Hut by mid-afternoon.

(Dick's diary, 29 December 1984, 14.00 hrs. The Saddle.) N, P + I a bit slow at getting to lunch-spot. About 2 hours late. Poor girls all cold. But sun v. bright. Sunburn could be bad. Bored too. Nick and I full of fun. We have all the excitement and rule the roost. We're OK. They said; 'You're OK. You're having all the fun. Let us have a go on the bikes.' Maggie and Michèle are masters now, not quite the power of our legs but nice legs all the same. Kate not as confident on rough stuff and yumps. We relaxed in the sun, happy to lie down and watch mountainbikes for a few minutes. Michèle pedalled off down the slope, skidded and fell over then picked herself up to find an even more tortuous route back.

Leaving us with some food, Kate, Maggie and Michèle then strode off looking very adventurous and promising to put up tents and melt some water ready for us when we arrived later. This was the true spirit of teamwork: a self-sacrificing support-crew prepared to give their all in order to provide tea and accommodation for the two heroic cyclists battling against the elements. Exhausted by our responsibilities, we slumped into the warm bowls of dust left by the girls, and turned our attention to an important issue.

'Where's the grub?' demanded Dick. We were sprawled, legs out, facing the sun, with balaclavas and scarves around our necks to keep out the cold. Dick rummaged in a rucksack and pulled out a plastic bag. It contained a packet of Ryvita, a bag of cashew nuts, some boiled sweets and the remains of his birthday cake, by now disintegrated into a sticky drift of multi-coloured crumbs.

'Isn't there anything to put on the Ryvita?' I moaned, dismally viewing the dry asbestos-like pieces of crisp-bread.

'Peanut butter. There's a jar in my pack.' With the deftness of a starving squirrel who's suddenly remembered where he's hidden his best nut, Dick rolled over and out of his rucksack straps, snapping out the buckles and plunging in a hand to withdraw a container-full of his favourite food.

I felt ill just looking at the muck-brown stuff. Dick loves it, and had been seen mixing it with jams, cheese, currants, bananas and digestive bisuits. All at once. In fact if the substance is remotely edible, he'll mix it with his 'PB.' These ingredients are not just piled on haphazardly, but applied in a structured fashion, with the 'PB' extending in uniform thickness to the very edges of the base material, and layers of 'complementary' foods built up on top into a colourful stratification. One of the many useful things that Dick's doctorate in sedimentology taught him, was how to find pleasure in order. Having constructed such a perfect layering, he eats it by carefully dismantling each stratum, rather than taking a big bite right through the whole lot. By contrast, my sandwiches often looked like particularly grisly motorway accidents.

Of course all our food had to be divided up equally; exactly equally. All parties involved in the share-out had to be happy that the total calories in each person's pile were precisely the same, and we often went to some lengths to ensure fairness. Dividing the Ryvitas was easy: there were three each, with the crumbs in the packet for Dick because his biscuit had a broken corner. The peanut butter was slightly more tricky, and could only be measured in 'standard smears;' since I hated the stuff, and we had several more gallons of it in various rucksacks I didn't find the division of this as important as the cashews, which were in short supply and much favoured because, unlike most of our expedition food, they had a taste.

All the cashews were emptied onto the lid of the plastic box and shuffled into three roughly equal piles. These were then redistributed into pyramids. We debated the relative sizes, standing up to regard the area covered from above, getting down on all-fours and sighting the piles horizontally to check that their altitudes were equable with total surface areas. A nut or two would be shifted from one pile to another, and everything re-checked. With no impartial observer to arbitrate, we could only wait for a consensus before declaring the piles equal. After considerable agonising and despite many re-allocations of nuts, and even half-nuts and nut-fragments, it wasn't possible to decide the issue on a merely visual basis, so we ended up counting the total number and dividing by three. For several dangerous seconds, group harmony hung in the balance when it was realised, even after a re-count, that there were 223 cashews.

'There's going to be an odd nut,' Pete said wearily.

'Well,' I consoled him, 'At least it won't be alone!'

White-Out

'Do you know', I asked, reading the label on the Ryvita packet, 'how many calories there are in each slice?'

'Twenty-six,' Dick guessed accurately. (He spends a lot of time reading food packets because, he once told me 'they cost less than newspapers and tell you more'.) 'And that's about 5,474 calories less than we need for a whole day!'

Thus fortified by a lunch which would have left a slimmer feeling peckish, we bundled our bits into packs while Pete snapped a few photos. Dick handed round a tube of UV cream, used to protect face and hands from the burning rays of the sun at high altitudes. With white streaks across our faces, we pointed the bikes towards Kibo. All being well, we'd reach the tents in a couple of hours. It was still sunny, but getting colder.

Before long the gradient began to steepen and we were reaching for lower gears. In places the trail picked its way across fields of small boulders, and we'd have to stand on the pedals, gently threading the front wheel through the lumpy obstacle course, hoping against hope not to fall off. Each re-mount was getting harder in the thinning air. We were cycling slowly, completely absorbed by the few feet in front of us.

Behind our backs a huge grey cloud was tobogganing down the slopes of Mawenzi and chasing its shadow across the Saddle towards us. We felt the sharp bite of cold wind, and before we could zip up our jackets the cloud was upon us and snow was driving horizontally across the trail. We stopped and fumbled with suddenly cold fingers to tighten draw-strings around our necks and sleeves, and to pull up hoods. It had gone very dark, and we had to lift our goggles to see. Ice crystals stung our eyes, and we pedalled uncertainly onwards, leaning into the wild wind. We rode close together, taking it in turns to shelter behind the other.

It was about time we had some interesting conditions. We hadn't had to cope with anything very difficult yet, and pushing on in blizzards was something that both Dick and I felt at home doing. I was in my element. Pete was up ahead, bowed in the lee of an enormous rock trying to pull on a pair of madly flailing over-trousers. The problem with the bikes in this weather was that their big side area was catching the wind far more than if we'd just been on foot; it was a satisfying challenge trying not to be blown over.

(Dick) With difficulty we cycled on; all I was thinking of was reaching the safety of our tent and friends an hour or so ahead. Pete in the cold, strode on confidently and was enveloped in the mist. Nick and I were struggling, the headwind and uphill combining tc slow us dramatically. The wind tugged at my hood, and I tightened the cuffs around my mitts. From the gloom a figure appeared. Low flying snow and a bitter wind seemed to push him towards us. He had on skin-tight black leggings, a pale yellow single-skin jacket, a balaclava down over his eyes and up over his nose, and apparently very little else. His eyes peered out through snow goggles and behind him I could see nothing but the lonely path snaking off into the mist.

Richard König was the coldest trekker I have ever seen. His legs were quivering as he spoke. He could hardly form his words. I reached over and pinched together an opening in his Velcro jacket fastening. He was obviously excited by something and I asked him if he'd come from Kibo Hut. No, he said, he had passed it on his way down from the

93

summit caldera, but had not stopped there. I explained that we were heading there, and, if he was that cold, did he want to come too? At Kibo Hut we would have spare clothes and sleeping bags. No, he was fine. He had extra gear down below. Ah, I said, so that is where your friends are? No, wrong again. It turned out that he was alone. The tale grew more bizarre, because he had in fact come from the other side of the mountain. There he had left his main equipment cache.

Now he explained his excitement. It wasn't that he'd tried to get to Kibo summit alone, nor that he had met two lunatics rolling along in a blizzard on mountainbikes, but that he himself had his own mountainbike on the far side of the mountain.

The astonishing fact was that Richard had also planned to cycle up Kilimanjaro. Now the competition was exposed for all to see. Richard König had obviously abandoned his plan after a couple of days, but who else might be up there with bikes? Nick and I were only just in time to claim a first ascent.

The porters relate the story of the Japanese who got a racing bike up to Kibo Hut last year. The Park Warden, Mr Nassari, remembers turning two Australians away only a month ago. Nick and I know of two other adventurous Aussies, Tim Gartside and Peter Murphy, who had pedalled across the Sahara a couple of years back and had come very close to extending their mountainbike tour to include Kilimanjaro. It was only a matter of time before someone did the obvious, and tried to pedal up Africa's highest mountain. We wanted to be first.

Richard König's story became more and more bizarre. He had flown into Nairobi on 24 December, one day after me, and cycled all the way across the African savannah on Christmas Day, to Tanzania. Rather than add an extra hundred miles by pedalling around Kilimanjaro to the Marangu Gate, he had cut straight up the mountainside towards the Shira Plateau on tracks so rough that he'd had to carry most of the way. He'd camped at 13,000 feet, but then found pedalling so difficult that he left his bike hidden near his camp-site. That was two nights ago. He'd been in Africa for no more than three whole days, and alone had cycled 200 miles and climbed 10,000 feet. After leaving his bike, he set out on foot to scale the precipitous north-west face of Kibo summit, but was turned back by technical ice-climbs. He had then traversed around the mountain to the Marangu side, slept in a gully in his bivouac bag, and set out next morning to climb to the crater rim. He left all his auxiliary gear, including bag and food, in the gully. And his food was hardly exotic: just four litres of liquid to last him the four days. He made the crater rim, but was so late getting there that he'd been unable to locate Gilman's Point in the thick mist. He was now on the way down to his equipment dump.

As he turned to head off down the slopes into the mist and snow, he had just one hour of daylight in which to descend 2,500 feet to a pile of gear hidden behind a nondescript wiry bush two miles away in a south-south-westerly direction. We wished him luck, but as the Himalayan Acorns team from the Cheshire Regiment said in Nepal to Ados and I: '. . . we're glad to a man not to be going with him.' I reached out to shake his hand. He raised his cautiously and said 'Please don't shake too hard. My hands are too cold!' We stood a while and watched him disappear into the gloom: a tiny yellow anorak on shivering black legs. We needed to move ourselves to avoid a similar predicament.

While Dick had been talking to Richard König, I'd been half-listening, half day-dreaming, making micro-adjustments to my clothing to keep the snow out and warmth in. When we climbed back onto the bikes, the light had noticeably faded; dusk was approaching fast. Dick was leading; I had my head down, following his wheel tracks and imagining myself into a toasting kitchen sat before a bowl of spotted dick and custard. Then, through the layers of windproof hood and balaclava I heard my cousin shout: 'We're lost. The path's gone!'

It took a few moments to sink in. 'Lost?' I shouted back, wondering if I'd heard him correctly. We stopped and looked around. It was a near white-out, with snow sweeping through soup-thick cloud. 'We were on the path back there, then it went faint. Now, it's gone altogether. It's getting too dark to see anything. Have you got the map, or have I? Where are the torches?'

Some wretched fumbling in rucksacks produced the sodden, stained piece of paper. The squiggly lines on the map bore no relation at all to the slope that we knew existed out there somewhere in the murk. We were pretty sure there were no cliffs to ride over in the dark, but it would be tricky finding the Hut. If we missed it we'd be bivouacking out for the night, not dangerous, but without a sleeping bag at 15,000 feet, fairly uncomfortable. We just had to find the Hut. Quickly.

The Moonlight Shuffle

We knew from others' descriptions of Kibo Hut that it was fairly well hidden from view behind surrounding outcrops of lava. And although we had compasses with us, they wouldn't be much use for pin-pointing the Hut because we didn't know where we were to start with. In all probability the map hadn't got the Hut marked accurately either. At best the compass would head us in the right general direction.

'The easiest way out of this is to find the trail again, and follow it straight to the Hut.' But the problem was finding the trail. We split up, arranging to ride in sight of each other 20 yards apart, on parallel courses that should, we estimated, cut across the trail sooner or later. It was difficult to pick out ground details in the half-light, and my wheels kept being knocked sideways by unexpected boulders, or sinking into patches of loose gravel. Once, I thought I saw footprints, shouted for Dick to stop, and padded around the area looking for more. But they petered out on harder ground, and we resumed the search.

Minutes later, Dick called out; a small blurred figure on a bike in the cloud. He said he'd found the trail, and was following it. I squinted to watch him.

'It's going in the wrong direction,' I bawled into the wind. He didn't appear to hear, and rode on. Then I saw Pete near him, also searching. It was virtually dark now, and although the snow had all but stopped, the mist seemed thicker than ever. Worried that Dick and Pete would get sidetracked following the wrong trail. I turned on the speed, aiming to get ahead of them and hopefully locate the rightful way first. Sure enough, I'd only been pedalling hard for a hundred yards when I came across a wide spread of foot-prints curving off to the left. It looked good, but the gradient steepened, forcing me to carry the bike.

'Path over here,' I shouted. Heads turned in the distance. They must have heard. While Dick and Pete stood and waited, I trudged up the slope, bike weighing a ton on my back. Slowly but surely, the curve of my path was heading to join the other. Great, I thought; saved. If the two paths met, then we must surely be heading in the right direction. Probably I'd strayed onto the trail that heads obliquely across the Saddle to Mawenzi.

We all met at the junction. Ahead, the trail climbed, hopefully towards Kibo Hut. Behind our backs, the weather was changing.

The first hint came as we laboured upwards, and unexpectedly found ourselves

Beyond Gilman's Point the rock towers and steep drops made it too dangerous to ride the bikes.

with clearer views. The black outline of surrounding rocks became distinct once again, and we no longer had to peer at our feet to make sure we weren't going to trip over and get walloped on the back of the head by a mountainbike. Then, in a few startling steps, we walked out above the swirling dankness and into a stunning sunset. Below us cloud hung from the Saddle like a giant duvet, with Mawenzi as a headboard shining gold in the dying rays of the sun. 'That,' said Dick, 'is pretty neat'.

Clear of the cloud, we knew we'd find the Hut, and we stood quietly, waiting and watching as the day faded. A solitary ray pierced the whiteness below sending a defiant beam across the Saddle, and second by second, the snow-fields that streaked the ridges of Mawenzi lost their brightness and the whole mountain became a dark shadow in the night.

'At last,' I said, 'A chance to use the head-torches!' We'd brought with us a couple of very fancy and unusually powerful torches used by mountaineers, and fitted with lenses that could be rotated to provide varying thickness of beam. Dick had come across them in Black's outdoor shop in London, liked the fruity colours of the elastic straps, and acquired a couple for the expedition. They turned out to be among the most useful items we had. With the lamp tightly on your forehead, both hands could be freed for either riding the bikes or carrying them; and wherever you turned your head, the beam followed.

(Dick's diary, 29 December 1984, Kibo Hut.) In better spirits now we cut up towards the hut. Fading sun left a red glow on Mawenzi's rocks and an annulus of cloud encircled the lofty towers. Our paths were deep in darkness. Head torches on, we picked a careful way. Within minutes of the sun's closure of the day, a nearly full moon was shining down on us.

Sharp moon-shadows gliding beside plodding somnambulists. Weighted down by angular metal shackles around our necks, slowed by extreme altitude. Gasping for breath as a fearful dreamer of nightmares gasps when ghosts climb out of the cupboard. No wind.

We staggered gratefully into our encampment at Kibo climbing hut, nearly an hour after sunset. Food high on priorities. Effects of altitude dulled our appetites. We drank a lot of tea and Nick and Pete downed a bowlful of spaghetti and Protoveg. The girls and I could only nibble the edges of the pasta.

We're in a communal hut. Four walls, a roof and creaky floorboards. No water, gas or electricity. Tiny windows to keep out the cold. A couple of wooden benches and table. I wonder how they got this lot up here? Other trekkers sleep in a couple of side rooms. It's only 9pm but they will try for the summit tomorrow starting at midnight. They are, so K + 2M say, the same people that were at Horombo last night. We try to be quiet.

We ate in the darkened 'dining room' of the hut, by the light of a flickering candle. Kate was hunched in the shadows, quiet and unable to eat, having had a desperate last couple of miles up to the hut with Michèle. She'd been sick just short of reaching the hut, though the two of them had fortunately missed the worst of the snow-storm. Kate said she was 'feeling like death' and just wanted to go to sleep. She ate nothing that night. I felt embarrassingly hungry and went on to demolish a steaming bowl of semolina sprinkled with coconut.

Round the candle we had a conference about the strategy for reaching the summit.

We were feeling the altitude, drifting in and out of painful headaches and nausea. We would have to acclimatise to our present height before camping any higher. Nor would it be reasonable to try to go higher if only half the team were eating; the last thing we wanted was for people to start collapsing at 20,000 feet with dehydration and energy depletion. All the factors pointed us towards a decision to spend a second night in the tents at Kibo Hut, and make our summit bid in two days' time. The girls could use the morrow for resting, trying to regain appetites and sorting gear, while Dick and I carried the bikes up Kibo to the crater rim. Pete would come with us to take photos and to carry a rucksack full of camping gear, and the three of us would return in the evening to Kibo Hut. It was a sound plan.

There was a tenseness in the thin air up here. People had come here and struggled. Some had won; others had not. A small percentage of those who walk between the posts of Marangu Gate get this far; even fewer make it to Gilman's Point, and a mere fraction persevere to Uhuru Peak. The mountain made everyone hurt, whether they reached the top or turned at Kibo Hut. There was a piece of paper on the wooden table in the hut. On it someone had scrawled some unfinished lines beneath the heading 'Halfway Cave':

> In shade so deep I hardly saw his face,
> He watched my whiteness fight against the hill
> That breaks so many when they reach this place.
> A place where man meets icy white and souls
> Of those who could not, did not, find the will
> To go up to that higher, thinner air.
> A simple choice: to turn, or take the dare;
> Slide down with empty mind, or climb and find
> The apex of such worthy goals . . .

The others drifted out to the tents, while Dick and I sat up by the candle, trying to write.

(Dick's diary, 30 December 1984.) I have the luck to sleep in Michèle's tent. It is pitched on a slight slope. We're going to sleep with our heads below our feet in order to aid blood flow to our brains. This is a crazy idea which probably has no effect at all. We dreamt it up when some Australians we met on the trail earlier today discussed conscious heavy breathing to overcome altitude effects.

It's getting hard to write my diary. My head is a dull thump of tiredness and ache. It's pretty difficult to think up here at 15,000 feet. My eyes hurt. One forgets to breathe and almost blacks out. It's like having someone sticking knitting needles through your brain.

... and he marched them down again

None of us slept well that night. Sleep at this altitude had a distinct pattern: pass out through tiredness; sleep for what feels like just a few minutes, then wake with heart racing and lungs screaming for air; sit bolt upright hyperventilating till heart and lungs resume normal activity, lie down and pass out; wake with heart racing etc etc. The problem seemed to be that when in deep exhausted sleep, the lungs adopt the

Ten yards was often all we could manage at one attempt before we found ourselves
gasping for air.

Abrupt snow ridges forced us off the bikes, though the crampons and ice-axes we'd carried up the mountain proved unnecessary.

level of shallow breathing you'd be used to at sea-level. And before long your body is starved of oxygen and threatening a major close-down of all functions.

We had two tents pitched, on sloping beds of rough volcanic stones. Even half-way flat ground was hard to find around Kibo Hut. After much searching Pete had come across a terrace of stones and gravel for the big three-man 'Super-Nova' tent several hundred yards down a jagged lava flow. There was a fifteen-foot drop right outside the tent door, so we had to be careful during nocturnal excursions. It seemed to take ages for dawn to arrive, and at first light I was out of the tent, moving slowly and trying to regulate my breathing. Half-way up the slope to the other tent, I met Dick coming the other way. He, too, was wanting to be off up the hill. The sooner we got climbing, the sooner we'd be down again.

(Dick) Day Four on the mountain was spent walking every single step of the way up the rough scree slope above the Kibo Hut. This stretches from 15,500 feet to the Kilimanjaro crater rim at 18,500 feet. It is all loose gravel and boulders, and Nick and I did the whole lot with our bikes draped around our necks. All the way up, we knew that the intention was to dump the bikes and then descend back to the lower altitude of Kibo Hut for the night.

It seemed to take hours to get everything organised. Dick was busy negotiating with Nicas and Simon; Maggie and Michèle had mixed up some dried milk and added it to bowls of muesli, which then stood in the sun hydrating into a khaki-coloured sludge. Pete had made his way off across the lava to take some photos of the mountain. On the ground lay a big rucksack packed with camping gear which we were hoping Simon would carry for us up to the crater rim. Dick and I had our own rucksacks, and a bike each to carry. Kate was still in the tent, but said she was improving.

Already the first of the trekkers who had made it to Gilman's Point that morning were on their way down. They'd risen at 1 am, reached the crater rim at dawn, and were now fleeing for the lower slopes and oxygen. We always seemed so slow to move in the mornings. Things came to a head.

(Dick's diary.) Knackered. Absolutely knackered. But also outrageously excited. We've just come through the most hilarious escapade. None of the porters wanted to carry our big rucksack. Not at any rate for a standard fee. They all demanded 2,000 to 3,000 shillings, the equivalent of 30 or 40 days' wages. As a matter of principle, we were not going to bend to that. We went off to find Simon, the strongest man in the world, and also one of the friendliest. He always has a big smile. With a little persuasion he agreed to 300 shillings, which is the equivalent of four days porters' wages, or two days for a guide. As he came out of the porters' hut, the others mocked him. He hesitated, looking at us, then turned back into the hut. His fellow porters would have made him a blackleg if he'd done the carry for us for less than the general demand. The porters all thought they had a monopoly over carrying our gear, and that for us to get that rucksack to Gilman's Point, we would have to hire one of them at their rates. They had another think coming. I unshipped my bike from my neck, took off my medium-sized rucksack and put on the heavy porter's pack, then re-loaded my bike. As I stood smiling at the porters, Nick went a step further by throwing off his bike, picking up my personal rucksack and strapping it on his front, putting his own sac on his back, and balancing his bike above

the whole lot. We set off very slowly, past thirty bulging eyes, in absolute silence.

The loads were excruciatingly heavy. We moved very carefully and deliberately, without stopping while in view of the hut. We knew they would all be watching, waiting to see us crack. I'm writing this at the first secluded hollow. It's taken well over half an hour to reach here, without a rest. Well worth it. We've shown the porters a thing or two, and I expect that, bicycles or not, they'll remember this incident for a long time to come.

We have discussed loads with Nicas and now he has offered to carry the rucksack for a reasonable fee and the possibility of a pair of our boots after the trip, so long as we don't tell the other guides he did the carry. So no-one must read this diary. It's worth noting how low the wages are here. A standard porter's wage is £3 sterling or about two packets of cigarettes in the U.K. The 300 shillings which Simon asked for would only have been £15 on the official rates. A black market operates, and hard currencies are worth five times as much.

We'd made our face-saving, half-hour speed ascent without turning our heads, and without speaking. The combined weight of the rucksacks and bike was fantastic. When we reached the first out-of-sight hollow, Dick burst into gales of laughter. Even Nicas saw the funny side of it after a while. I was so well strapped into rucksacks and a bike that they had to help me get untangled before I could stretch out and smile blissfully as a warm sun soothed a screaming body. There was pleasure in the absurdity of carrying bicycles up a volcano.

(Dick's diary, 1 pm, Halfway Cave.) Heavy duty. Hard work. We're slogging on. Halfway Cave now. A shady recess in the rock. So called because it's halfway from down to up, or vice versa. Twenty-minute breather. The slope is steepening all the time. Nicas has pointed out a little kink in the skyline above which he says is Gilman's Point. I don't believe him. I personally would be amazed if we can see the pinnacle of GP from 1,500 feet directly below.

The views are becoming superb. We look out over a mass of clouds covering East Africa, with only Mawenzi's black spires poking through. We are nearly level with their tops now. Nicas' brother is a master guide, who has once been up Mawenzi. Only once. The 'easy route' is a 2,000-foot steep snow gully. He hated it. I wonder what the harder routes are like?

From Halfway Cave onwards, existence became very simple. No conversation. No admiring the view. Just stare doggedly two feet in front of your own dusty boots, concentrating on making the end of the next zig before pausing for sixty seconds and attacking the zag. In an obtuse sort of way, I was really enjoying it. The pounding head and pained lungs were discomforts, but they weren't going to do us any harm. Mentally, it was very relaxing, with the extreme effort of the occasion chasing out of mind all those busy little problems that had been occupying us for days. And for once we didn't even have to worry about falling off the bikes.

We walked in each other's footsteps, taking it in turns to lead. Hol had christened this system 'the train'. He'd introduced it in northern Scotland when we'd be setting out in the dark for a distant peak, maybe walking for three hours or so before getting to grips with the mountain. Mountaineering in the dark can be tiring, and to preserve energy he had us moving in single file, feet following precisely the feet in front. Only

The last big climb.

the lead man had to concentrate; all the rest could virtually doze till daybreak. 'The train' works with groups of two upwards. Following Dick was easy. If I saw his feet slide, I could place mine correctively and avoid the same problem; saving energy; day-dreaming. It was all very pleasant. Pete brought up the rear, lending encouragement and photographing our backsides.

Near the top, the gradient steepened. Shale gave way to outcrops of rock and we had to scramble with the bikes balanced on our shoulders. Life became harder. We were at 18,000 feet. My head was throbbing with pain, legs and back aching, and I was easing the effort by complaining at every opportunity. We had on goggles to protect our eyes from the sun, but even these seemed to let through a searing surfeit of light. I walked parts with my eyes closed.

(Dick's diary, 4.30 pm. Crater rim just below Gilman's Point.) Worth every minute of effort. That 'little nick in the skyline' which Nicas pointed out is truly Gilman's Point. A six-hour slog, but now we have got the bikes up to the crater rim, ready for tomorrow's final effort. The route along the ridge to Uhuru looks promising from here—jagged but there appears to be a way. There's a wide snow-slope just before the summit plateau, which we should be able to ride up. Views superb. Wind light. Hands cold. Toes numb. End of Nick's nose rosy. Nicas is keen to set off down to the warmth and shelter of the hut 3,000 feet below. I'm happy to go now, so we get a good sleep at reasonable altitude before the excesses of tomorrow.

Dick lifted his bike over a rock, and snuggled it into a crevice for the night. I jammed mine on top, hoping they'd come to no harm while we were away. Looking around it was hard to see quite why anyone would want to snaffle a bicycle at the top of a volcano, but the London theft neurosis was by now a virtual instinct. I was feeling too smashed to admire the view, and decided to save it till tomorrow. We weighted down the expedition rucksack with a rock, turned and skidded down the scree. We were back at Kibo Hut before the sun set.

(Dick's diary, 8 pm, Kibo Hut, 15,500 feet.) A good day's work done. Not much of interest has happened. All slog and no cycling. No fun. At least the bikes are in the right place for tomorrow's final leg. Everyone is optimistic. Michèle and Maggie took a short walk today. Kate is looking much better; she's even made a flower out of waste-paper to brighten the supper table. Pete lugged his camera gear all the way up and then all the way back down with us. Mad fool. Everyone else at Kibo Hut went to bed hours ago in preparation for the midnight start. Michèle tells us that a group of trekkers from Exodus have pledged an I.T. donation. Possibly the highest charitable gift in the world. That's great. Only another £6,800 to go!

We're still preparing equipment. One tent, some food, emergency clothes, rope and ice-axes are already up at Gilman's Point. Now we must sort out torches, crampons, stove, a pan, a couple of spoons, sleeping bags, Karrimats, plus minor items like lighters, penknives and a compass. We need two more torches for emergencies. I'll have to try and buy some from Nicas or other trekkers.

I've made a small bag up of emergency medicines for cuts and bruises. The serious items such as Lasix for pulmonary oedema and Streptotriad for bacillary dysentery can wait down here. It's too dangerous to take them up with us because probably none of us will be in sufficiently good condition to make a safe decision about their use. Our backup is that if anyone feels worse than a rough headache and slight nausea, then we descend immediately to Kibo Hut. Once back to normality we can decide which drugs to administer, or whether to descend still further.

The Diamox really seems to work, and I have had the most rapid acclimatisation ever. It makes fingers and toes tingle, as though it really is thinning the blood or dilating arteries and veins to supply more blood, and hence oxygen, to the tissues. I think it's a drug which eases the processes at the root of altitude sickness rather than suppresses the symptoms in the way that headache pills do. Must remember to thank Dr Townend.

While Dick was playing with bags of pills and filling everyone with confidence by asking how much crepe bandage you need to hold together a broken leg, the rest of the hut was cluttering up with small piles of clothing, food and equipment. It reached its most chaotic state at about 9.30 pm, at which point there was a unanimous declaration of exhaustion, and the final packing was left till 'morning'. Since we had to be marching by 3 am at the latest, that would mean waking up at midnight . . . two hours' time. It wasn't the first time that Dick and I had embarked on a 'whopper' with hardly any sleep. Before the 42-hour non-stop bike and running jaunt around the three peaks of Ben Nevis, Scafell and Snowdon, we'd had 4 hours; before the mountainbike circuit of the Welsh 14 Peaks, we'd had 8 and 3 minutes sleep respectively.

I scrambled clumsily down the rocks to our tent, pausing on a ledge part way to turn and look at Kibo shining bright in the moonlight. Its slopes looked ridiculously steep for cycling. Up there, somewhere above those ice-fields must be Uhuru Peak. And in Wajir at that moment the camels would be settling for the night and the brush-wood shelters would be quiet but for the occasional cough. Tomorrow was going to be the real test; the culmination of all that effort and the day we must not mess up. I looked away, and felt the cold.

The old snow near Uhuru Peak was hard-packed and made for fast exciting cycling.

Three Miles High

At 12.30 pm the alarm detonated. My brain short-circuited as I tried to remember where I was. Nerve-endings felt as if they'd been pulverised in a food-blender. The prospect of emerging from the languorous sanctuary of my down sleeping-bag was appalling. It was pitch black, the outside temperature was well below freezing, my head ached dully, and I had to blink repeatedly to moisten dried and weary eyes. I felt like going back to sleep for another 24 hours. It was times like this that invited the question 'Why keep doing this? Give it a break mate! Take up something civilised like stamp-collecting and telly.'

For enduring the first ghastly minutes of days like this I'd developed over the years a technique: I tried not to think. Driving negativism from a pained brain by blowing the first few bars of the '1812 Overture' through pursed trumpeting lips I self-ejected from that fetid old sleeping bag, rubbed some refreshingly-cool tent condensation onto my face, sucked in a couple of delicious draughts of pure mountain air. And collapsed into a hacking paroxysm of coughs. I slid back into the bag and lay still, pretending nothing had happened. For a few blissful seconds sleep once again claimed me.

A stone turned outside. Gravel crunched. Bleary distress: Dick's arrived. I was out of the bag again and fully dressed (not difficult since I was sleeping in all my clothes) before Dick had got the tent-zip more than half way up. He was wearing a headtorch. As I stuck my head out it blasted me right in the retinas. What a way to wake up. 'Morning, Richard,' I managed cheerily. 'How about pointing that thing somewhere else.'

'Crimbals, aren't you lot up yet?' The boy sounded authentically dismayed for someone who had overslept by exactly the same amount of time as I had.

'Yeah, we're all up in here (I probed about with my feet to produce some grunts from the tent's other occupants). 'Just getting the gear sorted out.'

I dragged myself out into the night.

'Wassatime?'

'1 am. Got to move quick.'

I uncharitably began to collapse the tent before the others had emerged. We'd be carrying the 'Super Nova' up with us today, so that there'd be space for everyone to camp on the crater rim if the need arose. By 3 am we'd all got our packs loaded, and with Nicas leading, set off up the now familiar slog to Gilman's Point.

(Dick) We plodded in silent single file, close behind each other, heads bowed as though in reverence to some gods up there. Only the leader, Nicas, was aware of the world. We followed hypnotically, with total faith in his control. A strange feeling of déjà-vu. The pre-dawn starts with us lined up behind Uncle Hol on Scottish mountains. My thoughts were: hard work. We're ploughing the fields and sowing the seeds before reaping the bounty. Walking on, walking on. Each is cocooned in his own little world. The darkness all around, and total absence of wind enhances the isolation. Plodding on, plodding on. I pull my balaclava lower over my brow. All I can see are the stones under my feet.

My mind wandered a while ago to the drudgery of the Third World. All those people slogging day in day out. Hoping for a light at the end of the tunnel. Turning the soil; growing crops; building irrigation; making clothes; herding goats; fishing. Their work is hard work. They are the lucky ones. They have work. Many millions more have no jobs at all, no prospects, no future to mention. Trapped in the whirlpool of poverty. All they need is tools and equipment. They have the will and the muscle to work.

Like the young gent at Kibo Hut. He has the will and strength to climb to the summit, but being sick several times in the night, his body is not willing. Come to think of it, there are thousands back in GB who would be eager to have the chance of climbing Kilimanjaro but they have not got the finance. It's always a difficult question of how far to spend one's earnings on oneself and how far to spread it around.

Nicas, Simon and Solomon are relatively well-off for this area. They have lucrative foreign work. I wonder how they were chosen. Was it the autoselection we see in Britain where only the strong push through? 4 am passed behind us, then 5 am came and went. All the time we moved with short steps. Nicas in charge. We're in the dark sharing out peanuts. Maggie is feeling the cold. Kate is keeping up strongly. Michèle and Nicas seem to be chatting about something. Nick and Pete are quiet. That makes a nice change. They're moving steadily and strongly though I expect that they are submerged in physical and mental fatigue after the exertions of yesterday. I feel the same, saving all my energy and activity for the summit ridge. Only Nicas is wide-awake doing his job.

We had to use torches, picking our way carefully over boulders. It was bitterly cold, and the temperature dropped still further as we climbed higher. Dick's thermometer told us that it was −10 degrees Centigrade. Nobody spoke, and we rested for ten minutes every half hour. The eastern sky began to lighten after we left Halfway Cave, just a hint at first, then an orange glow which diffused and splintered across the horizon to set fire to the distant plains. Above Mawenzi rested anvil-shaped clouds which gently lifted and faded with the coming of the sun.

The last few hundred feet were agony: a tortured plod, pulling on the rock with hands; feet sliding; muttered curses. When finally the sun exploded over the crest of Mawenzi it flooded our awesome stage with unwelcome light; in the dark there had at least been a cosiness in which we could suffer privately. The frozen mountain beneath our feet reflected a warm redness which added to the uncomfortable contradictions we were suffering: a volcano covered by ice, frozen to the bone in the heart of hottest Africa, chronically thirsty amid all this solidified water, rock-climbing on bicycles . . . I heard Dick say to himself 'This is diabolical!'

Left: Altitude headaches and intense glare reflecting off the snow plagued us all along the ridge.

Above and below: Spectacular cycling high above the clouds under a brilliant blue sky.

Up to the Edge

We scrambled up the last steep rocks to Gilman's Point. Reaching the crater rim of Kilimanjaro is rather like climbing up the outside of a tea-cup. At the end of a long and slippery ascent you find yourself teetering on the lip, with an enormous drop a few feet behind you, and a no less fearsome plunge down into the crater just in front of your toes. At 6.05 am that morning we peeked over the edge. The snow-filled crater bowl was tinged with tangerine light and in the distance serried steps of the ice cliffs climbed towards the horizon. We were at 18,500 feet, the highest I'd ever been. Nicas said a brief farewell, shook our hands then turned and scampered back down towards Kibo Hut.

(Dick) We dumped the rucksacks on the ground and scrambled over the rocks to rescue our beloved bikes from their crevice.

'They're over there, just inside the crater lip,' I yelled.

Nick stepped a little closer to the edge and searched.

'There!,' he shouted pointing. 'Look at that glint.' A wheel rim and shiny brake cable nestled amongst the rocks and snow. My heart missed a beat. It was like being in love. The glint that Nick saw could have been the glint in the eye of a fairy princess.

They had weathered the night of enforced separation well. The scratches and knocks were a legacy of earlier days, and like Nick's eyes, they were glazed over; dusted with ice. Tyres were still rock hard, probably at slightly over 40 psi in the rarified low-pressure air, though there would be some compensating reduction in pressure caused by the low temperatures which make air contract. As Nick said at Kibo Hut: 'All the practising with different tyre pressures to suit varying terrain will mean nothing up there. It's a survival ride, with no stopping to let out air for icy sections, or pumping up tyres for the snow. We'll need all our energy and brain-power for getting to Uhuru.' All bearings were free and smooth running; the temperature has to be way below − 30° C before oil can freeze, and we were only expecting temperatures of − 15° C.

While Dick was fiddling with the bikes, I was fretting about survival gear. Each of us would carry our own equipment and spare clothing, so that we could survive alone in the event of an emergency. We'd be riding in our big Scarpa Trionic boots, whose special soles could grip well on ice and rock, with long woolly socks, thermal long-johns and our thermal salopettes to keep our legs warm. I wore gaiters as well; with my record of falling off bicycles I intended to keep as much snow out of nooks and crannies as possible. On our tops we chose thermal vests, an I.T. T-shirt, and our Berghaus Gemini double jackets. I had on my sister Fiona's woolly jersey but Dick opted out of an extra warm layer in the expectation of profuse heat generation when the cycling started. Both of us needed snow-goggles.

Each pack contained a bivouac bag, Goretex over-trousers, spare socks, T-shirts, duvet jacket, spare gloves and balaclava, compass, head-torch and food. Tied to the outside of Dick's and my rucksacks were a pair of crampons and an ice axe each. We also had a climbing rope and emergency sleeping bag between the two of us. We were kitted out for the worst eventualities. If the route to the summit turned out to be ice, we could rope ourselves and the bikes to rock outcrops, or belay ourselves to the ice using the ice-axes. And we had just enough clothing to survive one night in the open,

114

so long as we could dig a snow-hole in which to shelter from the wind.

(Dick) Recovering the bikes and sorting gear used a good half hour at Gilman's Point. Nick and I needed to cover all eventualities for the attempted ride along the rim. We could see much of the journey ahead. Jagged narrow snow-draped ridge leading to snow rampart and then formidable cliffs of Uhuru summit. The unseen dangers were the most threatening: fragile cornices, loose rock, ice crevasses and of course our own folly.

The others were keen to be off. The girls feared that their attempt would be slow and intermittent. They set off slightly ahead of us. It was tough for Pete since he had to hang around with us pretending to take interesting photos, even though the best photos were up ahead as we cycled over the ridge.

The time was nearing 9 am when we finally got our act together.

The three girls had already gone as high as most people on Kilimanjaro—Gilman's Point is regarded as being the usual turnaround point—they were all keen to try and reach Kilimanjaro's true summit, Uhuru Peak, as well. So they set off independently, and we hoped to meet somewhere along the route.

Uhuru

Dick was eager to get moving:

(Dick) I took a deep breath of anticipation and bent to grab the chunky black handlebar grip and leather saddle. This was the second start of what was undoubtedly going to be a very long and arduous day. It also promised to be rewarding. We had two miles of crater rim to traverse, climbing 1,000 feet to the highest peak of Africa. I pulled my bicycle upright and straightened my back. The handlebars looked cold and angular; ready for a tussle. I glanced at the pedals: mean rat-traps waiting for a real test. My legs felt weak already. I tightened the drawstrings on my waist and tucked in the cuffs of my gloves. A cold shiver ran down my spine.

Nick was already climbing on his bike. I bounced mine to shake off the snow, and wriggled my shoulders to get my rucksack comfortable before hoisting my leg over the saddle. By the time I looked up, Nick was sprawled on the ground. Downer Number One of the Bicycle Summit Bid 1984. His bike was out of sight. He rolled over, sat up, and burst into laughter.

The first few minutes of that ride were fairly light-hearted. Euphoric at the prospect of trying to ride a couple of bicycles around the snowy rim of a volcano at just under 20,000 feet, we put a lot of energy into the early yards. The weather was perfect: blue sky, with no hint of cloud or wind. Down below us was the floor of the crater, from it rising several dark volcanic mounds. The crater rim itself, along which our route lay, undulated into the distance. The early part was formed by a number of rocky spires, with a beaten trail of snow clinging tenuously to their bases. Beyond, we could see the soaring curve of dark volcanic cliffs rising towards Uhuru Peak, their jagged edge overhung by a long curling cornice of ice; we'd have to be careful not to ride the bikes too far to the right.

Uhuru Peak, at 19,340 feet, New Year's Eve, 1984.

(Dick) I was starting to get an altitude headache. Not yet serious, but enough to be distracting when resting. Nick got back onto his bike. We had lowered the saddles to a minimum, to make it easier to put down our feet when we felt the bikes going over.

Nick got his feet on the pedals and his bike took off down the slope at an alarming rate. I gleefully followed. When I next looked up, he had only gone fifteen feet. The trail had turned up; he had made a slight misjudgement of the angle, and steered into a deep soft snow bank. I whisked past, clipping his boot as he lay on his side, got three feet further before slamming my brakes on tight as I skidded down a slight undulation, both wheels locked. I glided gracefully across the ice for another few feet before the bike leant gently over and plopped me into the snow. All good clean fun. Harmless so far . . . but exhausting. We had covered twenty yards in fifteen minutes and now lay panting. We decided to carry at least part way over these very twisty ridges till reaching the smoother snow beyond.

I grabbed my bike firmly by the cross-bar and down-tube, and hoisted it vertically into the air. Gently I lowered it over my head until it snuggled into place and my body was bonded to the weighty angles of high-technology steel and aluminium. All the anguish of yesterday's 3,000-foot scree-slope slog came flooding back. Memories of slithering about in the mud of the rain-forest welled up. Once more into the breach. I resigned myself to the coming discomfort and took the first of many slow steps.

Our mood changed. The ecstasy of those first few pedal revolutions along the high snows evaporated. It was going to be extraordinarily hard to ride at this altitude, and it seemed that we'd be thrown from the bikes every few feet. Our way snaked out in front of us, picking a delicate line along the inside of the crater, just below the rim. This wasn't an established route; not many people make the trip from Gilman's Point to Uhuru Peak, and we were following a narrow trough of footprints which had fortunately stamped down the snow enough to form a usable trackway for cycle tyres.

We were at least lucky with the weather. Wind and cloud would have made it near impossible to contemplate the traverse, and fortunately the snow was fairly fresh, deep and absorbing. When we fell, we'd normally just sink in; if there had been more ice around we would have had to use the rope all the time for fear of sliding all the way down into the crater. In places the drops beside our tyres were near vertical.

(Dick) Progress was extremely slow. Two Swiss climbers came past us on their way back from a summit bid. They were leaning heavily on their ice-axes, looked dead-beat and hardly acknowledged us. We moved continuously but slowly. Many high-altitude climbers like to take 8 to 10 steps at normal pace, then wait to rest and recover before taking the same number of steps again. They set up a cycle of exhaustion and recovery within themselves. We were convinced that 'Slow and Steady wins the race'. Heads down, in silence, we plodded nearly 150 yards before coming upon a more level, contouring section, which, at its end, swooped down into a col. We tipped the bikes onto the ground, and re-mounted.

The knobbly 2^1/2-inch diameter tyres which had performed so admirably on the gooey mud 10,000 feet below, had a tenacious grip on the firm snow crust. We pedalled gently and rolled, with brakes partially on, at no more than walking speed along the path and over the col. Nick was tempted to try pedalling up the steep opposite side. His legs revolved madly. He climbed only a short way before slowing to a standstill and putting *his feet on the ground, holding the bike upright. Then he bent over the handlebars.*

I couldn't resist the challenge and pedalled furiously into the slope. It felt like hitting a brick wall. I was panting for air; my thigh muscles were stinging like nettle-rash and my altitude headache thumped. I heaved once, then once more on the pedals, pulling up on the handlebars, and drew level with Nick's back wheel, coming to a complete standstill. I sank down onto the saddle without falling over, put my feet on the ground, and bent double over the 'bars gasping for air.

'Who won?' Nick croaked.

'Not me,' I sighed.

'Hell of a way to keep fit.'

It was important to try and ride the bikes every inch of the way; not part of the game to climb off before being knocked off. To a third party our fanaticism must have looked lunatic. Even if there was a chance to turn the pedals just three revolutions, we would laboriously climb on the saddle, turn the right-hand pedal to two o'clock, push off, wobble for a couple of turns till the front wheel got knocked by a rock or sank into deeper snow. Maybe we did it because each time we fell, we could lie prostrate in the snow for a few minutes, eyes closed, trying to forget the bikes, the cold, the headaches and nausea.

As bicycle rides go, we were out at the edge. There wasn't a lot of room for error. We needed each other to pull the ride off without risking an 'incident' and yet we were still, even at this altitude, competing with each other. It was a matter of honour to ride further than the other before falling off, and each triumph was chalked up on the mental score-board.

(Dick) The ridge became a series of long carries interspersed with short frenzied bouts of pedal-pumping which were normally terminated with a flurry of snow around two upended heaps of bright blue Goretex, with ourselves laughing weakly.

No-one has ever been to this sort of high altitude snow and ice environment with bicycles before. We knew that we were trying an experience novel to bikers. Was it the fact that it was difficult, dangerous and exciting that made it worthwhile? The snow slopes below stretched in places for hundreds of feet; elsewhere we balanced on the edge of precipitous drops. The air temperature out of the wind had risen to − 10° C, though in exposed parts it was much colder.

Beyond the pinnacles the path wriggled up onto the very crest of the rim, and we found ourselves trying to ride along the apex of a ridge which bulged smoothly with snow and ice. We were now creeping up towards 19,000 feet, and rocks which peeped through the whiteness became fewer and fewer; this part of Kilimanjaro is permanently covered by glaciers and snow. The reflected glare off the snow was intense, and even through dark goggles we were forced to screw our eyes into slits. Dick somehow found the time and initiative to devise an additional glare-guard for his eyes. He turned his balaclava back-to-front. 'Works real well' he said through a layer of polypropylene.

I tried not to look ahead, knowing that I'd be dispirited by the distance yet to cover. I knew we couldn't be more than half-way along the ridge yet. Every yard was becoming a huge effort. We came to a flattish area that at ground level you would

The team: (left to right) Pete, Kate, Michèle, Maggie, Nick and Dick.

have romped across on a bike without a second thought; but just climbing onto the saddle had me panting painfully, and I only managed a few feet of pedalling in 'one-from-winch' at less than walking speed, before I lost concentration, the front wheel wandered off course and completely disappeared into soft snow, pitching me over the 'bars. I lay there for ages, eyes closed, swaddled in a drift of embracing snow. Up here there were just too many things to concentrate on. You had to remember to breathe, to pedal, to balance the bike and to steer and to look ahead. I could manage four of these at any one time, but never the whole lot all at once. I'd just manage to get the bike cruising along successfully, then be walloped in the lung department by a massive oxygen debt because I'd forgotten to hyperventilate. Or I'd be so intent on breathing deeply that I wouldn't remember to turn the front wheel at a bend. A couple of times, I climbed onto the bike from one side, and fell straight off the other without pedalling an inch. Ahead of me, Dick was lying on his side trying to pull a leg out from beneath his toppled machine.

(Dick) I was feeling the altitude badly. The shortness of breath I could cope with, but the headache was merciless, draping itself like a fire-blanket over everything I wanted to do. I was drowsy and lethargic, and had to keep reminding myself of the goal ahead. It couldn't be more than 500 feet more of climbing; maybe an hour or so.

Ahead lay a smoothly rounded snowy buttress. It peeled off left for 200 feet down to vertical ice-cliffs beside the Southern Glacier. On the right it plummeted to the crater floor. Our way lay up the middle, away from those fearful drops. It had looked cyclable from below; now it looked difficult even on feet. It wasn't even worth trying to ride it, though part way up it did look as if the angle eased. We lifted the bikes for our final long carry.

We walked in each other's footsteps, the imprint of the boot ahead forming a helpful little step. This must be the final climb, and just over the skyline must be Uhuru Peak. Not for the first time, the desperate eagerness on the lower slopes to reach the top, had been replaced by a reluctance to actually reach it once it was close. All the way up the mountain, life had got more and more simple, our objective clearer and the clutter of normal life further away. To our left was the most enormous ice cliff running for hundreds of yards along the top lip of Kilimanjaro, its sheer walls threatening and unstable.

(Dick) I remember starting off up that final slope with head down, trudging along, wrapped in my efforts. As we slogged on I began to realise how close we were to reaching the summit. Our target of the past few months was close at hand. My spirits lifted and I noticed the glaciers around me and the blue sky. I said something to Nick. He replied with a witty comment and we started a light banter which trailed off into trivia. The content is not important, but the essence is that life was looking up. The light at the end of the tunnel was becoming brighter. We could forget our immediate woes and open out once again to adventurous thoughts. A big new problem was looming.

'What do we do next if we get to the top of this one?'

'Goodness knows. Cycle up Everest? Run the length of the Americas?'

'Swim the Atlantic? Climb the Berlin Wall?'

'Let's get up here first.'

We found a level stretch to cycle. The footprints we followed had crisped to form firm ruts which jarred our knees. Our muscles would have been too tired for this struggle fifteen minutes ago but now we could press on. Ahead some craggy black rocks stuck through the snow. A voice called out 'Hello, hello'. And another 'About time too'.

Michèle, Maggie and Kate were waiting out of the wind. They surprised me and I realised that there were other people than ourselves on the mountain. They had put themselves to great discomfort in order that the six of us could reach Uhuru Peak together. Their wait for $1^1/2$ hours had been bitterly cold and they must have had rotten headaches from altitude sickness. Their gesture speaks volumes for friendship on the mountains.

Together we set out for the final short effort. There would be no need to stop to catch our breath. Our headaches were banished. The excitement and adrenalin banished all ills.

It was important to Dick and me that we cycled the last bit up to the very top. Without saying a word to each other, we simultaneously leaned forward and stood the bikes on the snow. To our right was a rocky outcrop. Ahead a gentle bump that had to be the top. The snow was hard and compact; easy to ride on. Tiredness lifted, and very steadily and slowly, we met with Uhuru.

Above: The ice-camp at Gilman's Point just before dawn on New Year's Day, 1985.
Below: Pete, the patient photographer, alternately froze and roasted as he took photographs in sub-zero temperatures then rushed after his two victims.

Above: Before we descend, a last look towards the snows of Uhuru Peak.
Below: On Kibo scree at dusk.

Summit Riding

(Dick) Nearing the summit cairn. All excitement. The other four beside us. They clap and cheer. Sounds like a massive victory crowd.

New Year's Eve 1984. Summit Uhuru Peak at 19,340 feet on top of Kilimanjaro. The highest in all of Africa. On top of this 'bright and shining' mountain, we, The Highest Cyclists in the World, hoisted our bikes over our heads in celebration.

While Dick sat on his bike staring across the crater, I was numbly trying to absorb the moment. We had got so used to having the bikes with us, that we no longer felt out of place with them on a high snowy mountain. What I wanted, was to see those two bikes and their riders through other eyes, in order to catch the bizarre wonder of the situation. Here were a couple of bicycles on the top of one of the biggest volcanoes in the world. Nearly 20,000 feet up in the sky. This was a special moment in the history of the world. It could be a while before someone else would do something quite as silly.

(Dick) Nick jumped back on his bike for more circles of the summit. I pedalled off along the ridge and came back for a second entry. Kilimanjaro is 7 feet lower than Cotopaxi. I was thinking 'If Nick braced himself on those poles on the summit, I could climb on his shoulders, and I could get my nose to exactly the same height as my armpit was on Cotopaxi. Maybe if Nick would let me jump upwards off his shoulders I could actually get my head up to the same height.' But at the time, Nick wasn't keen on the idea. Actually, the figure 7 feet was appropriate because Hol had calculated that the extra energy required to carry the weight of our teddy-bear mascot up the mountain, was equivalent to climbing an extra 7 feet.

We cracked open a packet of Marsh's Original Glacier Biscuits to celebrate. Our taste buds were not, unfortunately, up to their best, but we munched the biscuits ceremoniously. We shared our one pint of water and toasted Adrian's son Jaro. Then we raised a toast to Steve Bonnist and Intermediate Technology.

Here we were way above the clouds, clear blue sky all around, nearly 20,000 feet above sea level, actually riding bicycles. It hardly seemed possible. I couldn't sense the full implications, and didn't know how long it would be remembered by others. I knew that to myself, this moment would outlive this year and would be a grand source of tales. Two men, two bikes and twenty thousand feet.

Pete nipped around taking photos. The ladies got out assorted cameras and executed a few poses. We all held arms and gave big cheesy grins. They'd be preserved for posterity in our family photo albums. There was a stiff wind blowing, but I couldn't feel the cold, and in the enthusiasm of the moment I stripped off hat and gloves and opened my jacket to reveal my Intermediate Technology banner for the photos.

We finished off our water, and knew we needed more to stave off the dehydration that goes with altitude. Melting snow would have to wait. There was so much to do and see. Beyond self-congratulations, there were views out all over Africa. We must be able to see the blue skies above Wajir and should be thinking of them now. Would they get their windpump? We must be able to see above Nairobi and sister Barbara's house. There were game parks, animals, tourists and millions of locals below.

Up here we stood on snow and ice in a biting wind beside glaciers. Clouds billowed up from the black rocks below.

I had a horrid sensation that Dick was going to suggest that we try something 'experimental', like seeing if we could survive a night in a snow-hole right on the summit. So after we'd been up there for an hour, I was eager to slip away to safer climes. We'd been keeping a close eye on the changing weather. Clouds had begun to boil ominously around the teeth of Mawenzi's ridge far below us, and we were now isolated on a white rounded island suspended 5,000 feet above a bed of fluffy cumulus. Dick made Pete take a photo of us pretending to mend a puncture ('Come on Nick, it'll be a good joke'). I wondered if he'd got cerebral oedema already. Kilimanjaro's summit is crowned by a collection of sticks and poles, plaques and an old tin box. It looks like a crashed supermarket trolley. Dick contributed to the incongruity of the situation by getting out his spanners on the snow. There was nothing in the tin box. More photos, then we turned and left. Kate, Maggie and Michèle set off ahead. Pete would stay with us.

Party-time

The journey back along the crater rim to Gilman's Point was not fun. We left the summit at 3 pm, expecting to make the thousand foot descent in good time, but things started going wrong in the first few yards.

(Dick) We started excellently, with a push off from the summit. We rolled across the gentle hump of snow, with the hunch-back cornice to our left, and some easy pedalling brought us to the tight left corner by the ice-cliffs. I saw Nick's back wheel hang out a drop too far. A flush of powder snow filled the air, then he corrected quickly up front. This brought the bike upright again, as his left foot went down to touch the snow. A cry of 'Caramba!' went up as his trailing foot unbalanced him and the front wheel slewed off to the right. His left leg crumpled.

Before I knew it there was snow everywhere. Knobbly tyres jumped up and then twisted and disappeared. A light blue anorak spun over to reveal dark salopettes. An 'Intermediate Technology' badge flashed away; a hand, a boot and a yell emerged from a welter of white. He couldn't fall far; there was a rounded hummock 10 feet below that would act as a long-stop.

Above: Nick bites the dust as we race down Kilimanjaro.
Below: The finish at Marangu Gate, with our guide Nicas in the centre and Simon on the right.

Too late, I saw the ice under my own wheels. My brakes were helplessly locked on—the wrong thing to do on ice. My tyres teased the snow ridges on each side then I was on my knees, then my back. I spun round, rolled over and careered into Nick.

There was a long drawn out moment of silence, then I said 'Bummer!'

Several seconds later after deep thought Nick said, 'Technical misjudgement'. 'Grade 3C veering to Grade 4B corner,' I observed, spitting snow out of my mouth and raising myself on my elbows.

A second later we exploded in laughter; a couple of fools sliding around in the snow on New Year's Eve . . . We looked at each other through our serious dark snow goggles and creased up again. We were full of ourselves, jubilant with our success, bubbling over with adrenalin and excitement. Next minute we were heaving with breathlessness, sucking in great lungfuls of the thin air, chests heaving skywards. Squeezing a bellyaching laugh among agonising gasps for energy.

It took a while to calm ourselves down. Time was getting on and we had to get a move on to get back to Gilman's Point. We must select a campsite and pitch our tent before sundown. Once we re-established a more moderate state of breathing, and calmed our heartrates to nearer normal, we could start to pick ourselves up. I screwed the snow out of my ears. Nick brushed his face down. A bit of cold snow dropped down my neck. And then we were back on the trail. Slower now. The excitement of success was more controlled. We remounted and rolled slowly in jerks squeezing the brakes. Legs nearly straight, weight backwards, clear of the saddle.

The temperature had plummeted with the sinking sun, and much of our way back now lay in the shade. The shadows we had blessed in the morning because they shielded our eyes from the painful ultra-violet, were now tunnels of chilly discomfort. Steeply down below our wheels, the floor of the crater looked gloomy and uninviting; an icy prison. If we slipped down there we'd not have the strength to climb back out again, and would probably freeze before morning anyhow. The snow that had been warmed earlier by the sun was now hardening into a glistening sheen that had our wheels skating about in all directions. On some sections where we'd been able to ride on the way up, we were having to shoulder the bikes, and tread carefully. Most of it was thankfully downhill, but there were a couple of crucifying upward scrambles that had us hacking for breath and holding bursting heads.

Dehydration and tiredness had robbed me of speech and thought, and a kind of survival auto-pilot had switched on: I knew what was necessary to make it back to Gilman's Point and last out the night in a tent at 18,500 feet. Take no risks, keep asking yourself whether your hands and feet are getting cold (frostbite always creeps up quietly), watch the clouds for a change in the weather, watch each step, only ride the bike where you can fall safely; watch the other person. This is no place to get separated.

(Dick) We came off the easy smooth slopes near Uhuru Peak, towards the ragged ridge leading to Gilman's Point. The ice cliffs of the Southern Glacier were dropping behind. Clouds were blossoming up below us. In places they fingered through the serrations in the ridge ahead. Down to our left the snow slopes fell away for several hundred feet past a black rock-wall to the crater floor. Ahead, beyond the ridge, we could see for hundreds of miles into the blue yonder.

129

The last bit was a tight snow traverse below the spiky crater rim. I thought it would pass quickly, as we scooted up and down the knolls and nicked behind boulders, but it became a long struggle. Our summit euphoria had faded and the headaches were back with a vengeance. We were dried out, and all the exhaustion of the past few days came rushing up to meet us. I remembered the Frenchman we'd met below 'Last Water', and how bombed out he'd looked. That was how I felt now.

Nick stayed ahead for all the journey back. Despite being 'Cyclists on Kilimanjaro', we hardly rode the bikes at all. We only mounted if the route went down a gentle slope for ten yards or more. And that rarely happened. I was too tired to bother. No-one would see us here. We had done our bit.

We got back to our equipment dump near Gilman's Point shortly before 5 pm. The sun was already low. Michèle and Pete had boiled up some water ready for us. That tepid juice was like nectar. We set about locating a campsite. Maggie and Kate had already descended to the relative comfort of the tents at Kibo Hut; like the rest of us they were cold, exhausted and overcome by an overwhelming urge to lie down in the snow and go to sleep.

Dick disappeared over the lip of the crater rim, leaving his bike lying on the rocks. We'd had what would have been a 'heated discussion' (if the temperature had been above freezing) in fact a grunted argument about possible sites for the tent. Dick was all for carrying the gear down into the crater, and putting the tent up on a snow-field we could see. 'It'll be sheltered from the wind,' he said, 'and in the morning we can ride the bikes inside the crater.' The logic was nearly faultless, the only factors standing in the way of this forward-thinking strategy were that there was a rock wall between us and the crater floor, down which we'd have to abseil with two bicycles and half-a-ton of camping gear ('Agreed, that might be interesting,' I conceded), and that, once down in the crater, we could not get out again in a hurry if someone succumbed to oedema during the night. 'Look' he pointed out correctly, 'if the wind blows up in the night, that tent is going to be the highest habitation between the Atlantic and Indian Oceans, and that's where it's going to end up if the pegs come out!' At which point he climbed over a rock and out of sight.

I fished the tent out of the big rucksack. Michèle was half-sitting half-lying in the lee of some rocks, curled as a wind-break around the petrol stove. Pete was looking for more clothing. Every now and again, I peeked over the cliffs to see where Dick had got to. He eventually came into sight. First one hand, then another, clawing over the top of a ridiculously steep ice ridge. I cupped my hands and shouted 'What's it look like for camping down there?' After a pause for consideration, a faint reply wafted back up the rocks: 'Not brilliant, the bikes won't make it'.

We finally settled for a sloping patch of ice and snow, the most level place we could find. It was right on the crest of the rim. The exposure was fantastic, but at least the views were good. Using ice axes and a snow shovel we carved out a platform for the tent. It was hard work in the thin air, but it warmed chilled bones. Ten hacks then a rest, another ten, another rest, and in twenty minutes we had the foundations for a home. It took a painfully long time to erect the tent. The wind snatched at the light fabric, and the pegs kept pulling from the snow. To help prevent the tent from taking off in the night, we tied on extra guy ropes, belaying them to surrounding rocks. We heaped snow against the fly-sheet and used the ice-axes as giant tent-pegs. Finally we pressed into service two of the most expensive and secure tent-securing devices we could find: a couple of Saracen mountainbikes.

Inside it was cosy and dark. Even little movements were excruciatingly exhausting and produced pounding heads. But it was New Year's Eve, and on this day of all, at least some celebratory effort has to be made. For toasts we melted some snow, and for a high-altitude banquet we had Country Vegetable soup and mashed potato. The soup slipped down a treat; the mashed potato set like concrete then froze.

Sunrise at the Ice Camp

It was still dark. The tent seemed to have shrunk in the night and the narrow slot I'd occupied at last light on New Year's Eve had disappeared. I was now jammed against the nylon wall, with seemingly only one elbow on the floor of the tent and my body supported by the down-swaddled body of my neighbour. I'd slept right through; quite amazing considering the altitude. The others seemed still to be sleeping. A persistent wind was tugging at the tent. I wriggled my toes and fingers; everything lovely and warm. We'd put the tent up with the door facing due east, so that the dawn of 1985 would blast straight onto us. 1985 is I.T.'s 20th birthday. I lay for a moment, worrying that if I went back to sleep, I'd miss the important moment, and that the sun would be a couple of miles high before I next opened my eyes.

I needn't have worried. An hour later, as he struggled to unzip the tent-door, Dick put his foot in my mouth.

'Wassgoingon?' I demanded in a muffled kind of way through a reeking and very hairy size 10 sock.

'Voices. I've just heard voices. There's somebody out there. I'm going to have a look.'

'Dick . . . are you all right?' I tried to turn over so that I could see his face. Maybe my cousin had got advanced hypothermia.

'I'm just going outside. I won't be a moment.'

In the semi-darkness I caught an expression of grim and resigned determination etched on the haggard lines on his face as he fought to drag a pair of frozen boots onto his feet. He lurched outside, clawing down the tent zip after him. I listened as his feet crunched out into that frozen deadly world. After several uncertain steps, there was a brief silence, then I heard the urgent deluge of several pints of processed soup hitting the snow.

That's when I heard the voices too: an abstracted excited chatter. I finger-bored an ear and shook my head. They were still there. Dick was right; there must be people out there.

(Dick) Several minutes before the dawn of the New Year, as the heavens started to glow behind Mawenzi to the east, I stepped out of the tent to breathe the air. The intermittent murmur of voices came through the wind and I looked towards the crater rim. A couple of heads appeared over the rocks and then several more. The first people to climb up from below to Gilman's Point in the New Year. They were presumably hoping to be the only group to see the New Year in, but raised a hearty cheer when they saw

131

me. I called to Nick and Pete and Michèle and we shouted Happy New Year in unison, and huge oriental grins creased their faces. Then they must have spotted not only the tent which surprised them, but also two bicycles. They flung their arms above their heads and yelled congratulations. Then turned laughing gaily for the last minutes before sunrise.

I wriggled back into the tent. My boots were rock-solid, and I'd only managed to get my feet half-way into them. The sky was lightening in the east and a red glow growing above Mawenzi. We left the tent-door unzipped and flapping. A shaft of light shone into the middle of our pile of sleeping bags. Presently it strengthened, changed from red to gold, and sliced across the tent: the first light of the New Year sun. We zipped the flaps up again.

A couple of short conversations and the effort of appreciating the sunrise sent us back to sleep for another hour. It wasn't till there were mutterings about thirst that the day got properly under way. Dick, being close to the door, was 'volunteered' to go and fetch a billy-can of snow so that we could make some drinks. This time he thawed his boots out over the stove, kneading the leather into acceptable suppleness. Accompanied by a lot of voluble whimpering and a camera, he departed once again, returning twenty minutes later with a can of ice-nodules and a film of 'ace pics.' He said he was feeling great.

'Happy New Year everyone' he said to three comatose sleeping bags. 'Bit of a change from traditional Brits who get drunk each New Year.'

'Too much of a change' came the pained response.

'I wonder what Hol's lot are doing right now?' They'd be up in northern Scotland, on An Teallach or camping out on the slopes of Sguur Something.

'Having some decent grub, if they're sensible.'

'Porridge.'

'Bread and marmalade.'

'Tea, chocolate, tinned peaches, custard. I feel sick.'

We had lost our appetites. Leaning out into the porch of the tent, stirring a can on the stove which was perched on a narrow shelf of snow, I started up a production line of insipid drinks. We started with tepid snow-melt and progressed through weak soup to stronger soup, and rounded off breakfast with runny mashed potato. We dumped a load of powdered tomato soup into it, which made it go all red. The 'Red Drinking Potato' was a smash hit, and we supped it for a couple of hours.

The subject hadn't been mentioned, but one of the reasons we'd camped on the crater rim rather than head straight down to more comfortable altitudes, was because we had always intended to have a go at riding the bikes inside the crater itself. This we reckoned was a one or two-day expedition in itself, with the attendant dangers of food and liquid shortage, and of over-stretching ourselves. As the hours passed, that plan was looking less feasible. I was being swept by waves of nausea and blinding headaches, and wasn't feeling either brave or adventurous. Secretly I was hoping that Dick felt the same (or worse) and that the crater-plan would be scotched.

(Dick's diary.) Lethargy is the big problem. I can't be bothered to move. No-one wants anything to eat. Kilimanjaro Teddy looks hacked off too. We've spent a long time getting up. Bouts of pretending to pack. Then stop for more sleep. We slept last night in

all our clothes; thermals, shirts, jumpers, jackets, trousers, socks, gloves, balaclavas, but in deference to respectability, no boots. We all have Ice Cap duvet jackets and down sleeping bags (I've got two) to keep us warm.

I'm jotting down some notes on this piece of paper. Nick and I have just finished an attempt to write The Sunday Times *report. Trying to think and write at 18,500 feet with the temperature several degrees below zero, is seriously 'over the top'. The report starts: 'Sunday Times (Happy New Year from Kilimanjaro) by Nick and Dick Crane . . . The mental effort required to write a conventional article at 18,500 feet with altitude sickness, and the air temperature* − 5° *C inside the tent (goodness knows how much lower outside) is way beyond the endurance abilities of us two. We are sending out a string of notes, half of which may be illegible or unintelligible, and hoping that you can piece them together into paragraphs.'*

I've had mountain sickness before. The headaches, nausea and loss of appetite are old hat. The effect of simply rolling over makes us, who consider ourselves pretty fit, breathless. But a new phenomenon to me is the extreme lethargy that's wrapped itself around us. By noon our heads hurt too much to consider anything strenuous . . . We couldn't stomach the thought of eating anything solid. I found some dates and peanuts in my pack which I thought might be tasty so I said 'Who wants some dates and peanuts?' No-one answered. Nick replied 'No thanks, but if you've got a moment I'll have a brain transplant.'

I'm lying in the door of the tent. My legs are still tucked up cosy in a sleeping bag, snow goggles over my eyes. It's midday. I'm finding it hard to believe that Nick and I were really up there on top of the highest mountain in Africa, just 24 hours ago. From behind the tent we can see the whole route up to Uhuru. I feel ready for some more sleep.

Michèle sat waiting all morning as Dick and I struggled to get some words down on paper for *The Sunday Times*. She had slept well but felt too weak to eat. Soon after midday we finished 'work' and Michèle set off down the slope to Kibo Hut. She was to be the first 'runner' in the chain that would whisk our photos and story down from the crater rim and back to London in the following day and a half. Kate and Maggie were ready at Kibo Hut to run the second leg. As she set off down the slope she called back, asking when to expect us down. Dick replied:

'Don't call out anyone till daybreak the day after tomorrow.'

The Great Crater Debate then fired up. Should we or shouldn't we spend two more days up here, stretching ourselves and resources still further. If we went down into the crater with the bikes, we'd be entirely on our own. It was a huge place. If we got into difficulties there would be no Mountain Rescue Team to pick up the bits. The weather looked as if it might close in, and we knew there had been blizzards up here over the last few days. Furthermore, since a visit to the inner crater meant a descent, it followed that when we finally did decide to turn for home, we'd have to climb up a thousand feet before we could get down; a grim paradox to contemplate. On the face of it, all these problems were surmountable, and there was every reason to go cycling in the crater.

We had all the right gear: ice axes, a rope, crampons, food and fuel enough for at least three days, and all our clothing and tent were still functional. Most important of all, we still hadn't written off one of the mountainbikes. Not to take the experiment

133

Setting off down the crater rim to Kibo.

further and to miss cycling into the heart of a smoking volcano was a pathetic bottling-out of the highest order. Unanimously, we elected to be pathetic.

The Descent of Man

Like drugged caterpillars we grunted, huffed and puffed in our sleeping bags, trying to get dressed up for the cold before leaving the cosy confines of down. Every exertion hurt, and we moved very slowly. Through our indecision we were, as usual, short of time, and already had no hope of returning to Kibo Hut before dark. Yet again, we'd have to equip and mentally prepare ourselves for the prospect of emergency bivouacs. We each checked our personal kit meticulously, making sure overgloves were in accessible pockets, and that we had the right combinations of thermal clothing.

(Dick.) We melted enough snow to provide us with water for the next descent. This added up to several pints of valuable liquid in plastic containers, which weighed a ton. Down sleeping bags, Ice Cap duvets, assorted socks and spare layers were packed away. Cooking stove, pan and cup were shovelled into a plastic bag along with unrecognisable items of half-cooked, half-eaten food, then the whole lot was dropped into the top of my rucksack. Karrimats were rolled up.

The tent was plastered in ice which added to its weight. When we'd got everything packed up, we found we had the biggest and heaviest loads we'd ever seen. Each of us had one of the huge Karrimor expedition rucksacks and one of the medium sacks to carry, both stuffed to the brim, with items like Karrimats and pans and bottles tied on the outsides. And we had the bikes on top of that. Nick put on his two rucksacks while sitting down, and found he couldn't stand up.

When we pulled our bikes out of the snow to make our conclusive exit from the mountain, the shadows were already stepping out from the crags. The sun was dropping down with increasing speed towards the black cliffs of Uhuru Peak. The air was very still. The blue above was totally empty except for the sun, and a pale moon which was climbing apologetically in its path. It was so quiet and calm that I could almost hear the creak of ice in the northern glacier, and the flutter of flags at the summit. I was sad to say goodbye.

We were leaving the adventure before we had really got started on the meaty bits. Our immediate objective had been fulfilled: that of cycling to Uhuru Peak. Unfortunately much excitement and experimentation with the bicycles had to be abandoned, partly because of our physical state, but principally because of the constraints of time in the modern society 3,000 miles away to which we were bound.

Whatever the misgivings, we had gone a little further along life's path and in doing so had learnt a little more about ourselves and a drop more about other people. It is only by pushing ourselves near our limits that we get to explore ourselves. And only by living under stress with others can we form true bonds. It was certainly sad to leave Kibo summit, but no doubt many adventures lie ahead.

I wiped a tear from my eye. The bright sun made me blink. I shed a few more tears.

'Shit,' I said. 'Help me Nick. I've got something in my eye. I need to get my contact lens out.' Nick was beside me in an instant. We crouched down in the snow, making a windbreak. He knows the agony himself, since he is also vain enough to wear these hidden crutches. I cupped my hand over my eye and flicked the lens out. Immediately I licked it up with my tongue and into my mouth. No doubt this sounds a strange ritual to many people, but in adverse conditions the safest place for a contact lens is in your mouth. There it is safe and clean because saliva is mildly antiseptic and the tissues of the mouth are sensitive enough to feel its presence. Cold fingers and hands, especially with gloves can't feel a tiny plastic disc.

I wiped the corners of my eye but had lost the irritation. I suspect that above the snowline, coarse flecks caught in the eye are in reality small grains of snow which are cold and angular but quickly melt. I massaged the lens with my tongue, spat a dab of saliva onto the end of my finger, pushed the lens from my mouth with my lips onto the finger and replaced it in my eye. The saliva sticks it to my finger and lubricates it in my eye. I've been doing this for 5 years now and have had no real problems. I don't recommend anyone else does it full time like me, unless they are keen to risk eye damage, but it is well worth remembering if you're ever vain enough and get caught out. (My contact lenses are hard. This technique must not be used for soft or gas-permeable lenses.)

Setting off down a mountain towards warmth and safety normally encourages a spring in the step and a whoop in the air. But at Gilman's Point that afternoon I was barely capable of lifting one foot above the other, and we'd given up conversation long before. It was too much hard work.

There was no chance of riding the first section; it was a serious rock scramble. With a rucksack on my back and front, and a bike on my head, it was impossible to see where I was going, and each step was a question of fumbling for unsighted footholds before transferring weight.

(Dick) The bikes kept jamming on overlarge rocks. The tops of some rocks were smooth with ice, and in between boulders were patches of snow alternating with loose gravel and rock flour. Any choice of route appeared to be wrong, and a couple of times we had to climb back up a section to find an easier route down. It took us till dusk to descend that first hundred feet.

'Not an appropriate way to make an exit from cycling up Kilimanjaro,' observed Nick. I nodded agreement. It was a shame to have to carry the bikes downwards, when we'd laboured so hard to get them up. This ought to be the easy bit. But at least we could ride them all the way once we reached Kibo Hut. We could just see its roof shining metallically, 3,000 feet below our feet. Just this slippery slidy scree to negotiate and we'd be off. I was calculating how long the plod would take, when Nick turned around and leant forward into the slope, letting his bike crunch onto the scree: 'Know what I'm going to do?' he said. 'Ride!'

Flying Finish

The irony of having to carry a bicycle *down* a hill was, even to brains which felt as if they'd been steeped in quick-setting cement, too much to bear—as was the weight of a velocipede and two rucksacks on bruised shoulders.

My first attempt at high-altitude freewheeling ended in spectacular disaster. The combined weight of rider, bike and rucksacks was over 130 kilograms; a lot for a pair of brakes to hold in normal conditions. I was sitting on the back rack of the bike, keeping the weight as far rearwards as possible on the 45° scree slope; I could just reach the handlebars with outstretched fingers. What I didn't realise until the whole ensemble was travelling at breakneck speed was that I couldn't see where I was going. The rucksack I was wearing on my chest had been pushed upwards into my face, leaving me totally sightless as the bike reached terminial velocity, hit a lump of lava and took off.

(Dick) I waited till the dust had settled to see if Nick was going to get up. He'd entirely disappeared in a great mushroom cloud. When it cleared, Nick was lying upside down and covered from head to foot in grit. His bike was several feet down the slope. I was already on my bike. I don't like to let a good chance to experiment with physical extremes escape me. Nick's method: feet on pedals, bum over the rear wheel, brakes on firmly, worked after a fashion, but it was hard work. My arms felt surprisingly weak after only ten feet. To impress Nick, and also to go one better, I decided to hang on until I was a few feet past him, before getting off for a rest. I took a line slightly wide of where Nick's legs were splayed out, adopted a racy pose with legs slightly bent and springy on the pedals. I just missed the knobble which had toppled Nick, but my front wheel suddenly dropped into a dip and I was over the handlebars. Rucksacks and I landed in the grit. Life was getting fun again. Here we were at 17,500 feet, playing BMX.

For several hundred feet we experimented with varying modes of downhill travel. Most ended with wild uncontrollable slides and somersaults. We looked like a couple of corporation dustcarts falling down a cliff face. Each pile-up was accompanied by fruity language, luggage breaking free and explosions of lava flour which hung in the air above the victim like bomb bursts. Dick, being annoyingly innovative as usual, was experimenting with forward-loading of luggage. He had a rucksack tied on his handlebars and another on the back, while he himself attempted to hitch a ride on the rear carrier. It proved a dramatic demonstration of the forces of gravity over friction. The bike turned over, end on end, and Dick's large expedition rucksack took off down the slope in a series of giant hops, with its owner bounding down after it shouting 'Crimbals! Crimbals!'

If the mashed potato had looked unpalatable at our ice-camp, I could just imagine what it would look like after it had been atomised over the inside of a rucksack. A hundred feet below me, Dick rugby tackled his errant luggage and the two of them slid to a dusty halt. Picking up Dick's abandoned bike, I wondered for a moment whether, with two bikes now at my disposal, I could somehow create a catamaran effect, and ride both at once down the scree. But it was just too difficult to balance. By the time I reached Dick, he had dreamt up the final solution:

(Dick) The fastest way of descending the scree was by not actually riding the bike, but using it as a wheeled outrigger. This may sound like cheating, in that it's not actually 'riding' the bike, but it turned out to be a very quick way of travelling down steep scree with a heavy load. You lie diagonally across the bike, legs out in the dirt one side, wheels churning the dust on the other. The bike's top-tube is tucked into your armpit, eyes peeking over the handlebars, and rucksacks resting on the saddle and rear rack. Following my near disaster with the disappearing rucksack, I had my two packs strapped to my bike then I strapped myself to the packs thus making a complete unit. The rear brakes are locked on, but partially released every few yards to prevent the rubber wearing through. The front wheel is allowed to turn like a slowly revolving ski.

Although I hated to admit it, Dick's monocoque slalom theory did seem to work. We tore down a thousand feet with a speed and verve that would make Jean-Claude Killy look like a dumper-truck on a nursery slope. With every foot descended we felt better. The crippling lethargy of the past two days was lifting, though the headaches were still there, drilling away at addled grey-matter. It wasn't our legs that finally gave out during this flying finish, but a far more sensitive part; a part that had been bruised and chafed on a leather saddle for too long – our right armpits.

It was agonising. The jarring and rubbing suddenly came home with red-hot fire and numb cries of 'Ggnnuunng'. It took quarter of an hour to swap sides, so that we could inflict the same pain to our left armpits. One more long slalom and it was time to stop for a rest. It was nearly dark.

(Dick) We stopped breathless to gaze down scree, and back up from where we had come. All around the evening was closing in. Gloves and balaclavas came out, and we zipped up our jackets. Nick put his head-torch over his head in preparation for darkness, and I got mine ready for use by clipping the battery terminals on. Nick then took his head-torch off again, clipped on his battery terminals, and placed it back on his head. Together in spirit, although slightly out of tune with regard to the speed of our mental processes, we set off.

Our antics on the scree were being observed from below. Outside Kibo Hut Michèle and a crowd of German trekkers were following our every fall through binoculars. The entire descent is visible from below, and in the fading light they'd watched the wisps of dust rise from the dark lava.

'What are they doing?' asked a newly arrived French girl, wrapped up in a thick duvet and mittens.

'Riding bicycles,' Michèle replied without looking away from the Zeiss eyepieces.

'Oh, I see.' The girl moved slowly away, looking at Michèle over her shoulder as if further contact would cause her too to start saying crazy things.

With the dusk came the cold, and the temperature slipped quickly below freezing. The watchers saw the two tiny figures halt for what seemed ages, then start out again, this time pin-pointed by two twinkling lights. Darkness wrapped itself around the mountain, and the two dots of light winked lower and lower. Somebody asked Michèle if the two cyclists would actually be riding their bikes, and she answered knowingly: 'I should think so. They're mad enough to try anything!'

Up on the scree, our high spirits had evaporated with the enveloping blackness. All we could see of each other was a wildly swaying beam of light, which sometimes pointed downhill, but more often than not veered wildly into the sky or across the surrounding slopes, accompanied by a muttered curse as yet another boulder was struck. We were each isolated in our own private struggle. In the dark it was harder to share the effort, and the problems seemed to multiply. I'd now tied both my rucksacks on top of each other, and they kept swinging to one side and pulling me over. It was driving me mad. I was cold, and couldn't be bothered to stop and unship the gargantuan load which I knew would take me ten minutes to get onto my back again. When I did finally chuck it all on the ground, my hands were so cold I couldn't get the rucksack straps undone. And I discovered that two of the Karrimats that had been tied to my load, had disappeared somewhere during the descent. Dick was down below me. He too had stopped and I could see his illuminated hands also fighting a rucksack. It was impossible to tell how much further we had to go; there didn't seem to be any light at Kibo Hut.

Dick waited for me while I slithered clumsily down the scree to him. Every few feet the bike seemed to pile into a rock and stop dead and I'd end up on one or both knees trying not to fall down the slope.

'Can't be much further,' was all he said.

The gradient soon eased, and more to liven things up than make quicker progress, we decided to have a go at riding the bikes. It was quite the most hair-brained idea. The head-torches picked out the rocks ahead, but our reaction times had slowed down so much that we'd be unable to avoid them. We scooted feet-down, managing a few feet-up sections once we got below the lava cliffs that stand above the Hut. Here the trail gets firmer, and we found that as long as we could control our swaying backpacks, the bikes could pick a safe line between the boulders.

(Dick's diary.) Helluva steep scree. A lot more fun coming down than going up. Rucksacks strapped to bikes. Many topples. Gravel everywhere, even in my underpants. Should be sorry to see the end of the expedition but right now I'm thankful for the back of the mountain. I hope there's Pete, Michèle and grub ready at the bottom.

Michèle had seen one light emerge at the bottom of the cliffs, and hurried over to the petrol stove, pumped it into life, and re-heated the jug of tea she'd had simmering for the past half-hour. A small knot of porters and guides had gathered in the cold at the corner of the hut, and were looking expectantly up the slope.

For us it was a wonderful moment. We found ourselves suddenly in sight of the hut's tin roof, and spurred on by its closeness we rode the last hundred yards without falling off, rounded the last bend and pedalled right into what at the time seemed a throng the size of a Cup Final crowd. People milled everywhere; there must have been nearly fifteen. Michèle bounded up bearing a huge aluminium jug in one hand and a plate of popcorn in the other. The jug was full to the brim with the best tea ever to grace parched throats.

(Dick) All was hugs and kisses. Nicas appeared, and squeezed in close to stand with his clients. Soda Enarc, the head guide came over and leant on my handlebars:

'You have made me proud. I have had nothing physically to do with your efforts, but I am pleased that you have done it in territory which I know well.'

'Soda,' I told him, 'You may not have been involved in this expedition, but it was an adventurous spirit like yours which helped us get to the top. Now this one's done, we just have to do the grand expedition to end all expeditions.'

'What will that be?'

'You tell me!'

It was still New Year's Day. Dick was eager for a 'proper' New Year's celebration. Apparently the 'drinking potato' had not been his idea of suitable lubrication. A bottle of whisky appeared and we were invited into one of the small porters' cabins, a cramped timber and tin building lined with wooden bunk-beds. It was jam-packed, with porters and guides sitting on every available surface. I was on a bottom bunk, sandwiched between Simon and a porter wearing a brown duvet jacket that sprouted stuffing at every seam. Someone's feet hung down from the bunk above by each of my ears. Dick was only just visible through the dense fog of cigarette smoke and fumes seeping from the wood-burning stove in the corner. It smelt as if they were cooking old boots. It was blissfully warm and comfortable, and everyone was talking at once. They all wanted to know what it was like riding the bikes between Gilman's Point and Uhuru. I eased backwards into the shadows, leaving Dick to tell adventure stories.

An Uninvited Adventure

Unsurprisingly, we woke late next morning.

I pulled on the same smelly socks which I had worn for six days, tipped the stones from my boots and put them on.

'Good morning,' I said to onlookers in general. Nicas came forward with a bright 'How are you?'

'Tired.' I replied, searching for an adequate expression to describe a dull and stuffy head.

'When will the others be up? I've been guarding the bikes. When will you be ready to go? Can I take a bicycle for you?'

I cottoned on. Nicas wanted to ride one of the bikes. Nick crawled out of his tent.

'Nick, Nicas wants to ride your bike.' Nick didn't reply. He was still half-asleep, on all-fours half out of the tent, blinking in the bright light and looking blearily at the scene. Nicas waited until all the other porters and guides were watching him, and then pushed

off confidently and headed downhill. He disappeared out of sight, freewheeling fast round the edge of a small hill.

Nick got himself upright.

'Where's my bike?'

'Nicas has gone for a ride. He went that way.' There was a moment of silence while the information sunk in. Through the stubble and sunburn a tinge of colour crept into Nick's cheeks.

'On my bike? He's gone on my bike?' (The voice was rising.) 'He might smash it up.' My cousin turned and sprinted off down the hill. He was wearing a suit of thermal underwear, balaclava and heavy climbing boots. I shouted after him: 'You haven't smashed it yet, so how can Nicas!' But he was out of earshot and running faster. A while later Nick plodded back up the hill. 'Where's Nicas?' I asked.

'Dunno. Gone. Out of sight. Couldn't keep up. My poor bike. Nicas might write himself off.'

A long while later, Nicas came back, pushing the bike, pleased as punch. He'd been a fair way down across the plateau, and proudly showed us a couple of cuts on his knee. He'd had to push the bike all the way back. The bike, much to Nick's undisguised relief, was undamaged.

The freewheel down from Kibo Hut to the bottom of the mountain promised to be fun: 10,000 feet of continual downhill over a mixture of dust, rock, river-bed, mud and finally hard-packed earth would be an exciting mix of terrain over which to take the bikes. I was looking forward to a lot of excitement and had the same kind of anticipatory thrill that I remembered from the start of a marginal rock-climb: you know everything will go fine so long as you don't lose concentration for a single moment. I wanted to ride fast.

But before the fun could start, we had to go through the normal chaos that surrounded the dismembering and packing of our camp. Tents had to be collapsed; that was the easy bit. Then clothing, Karrimats, crampons, ice-axes, rope, stoves, pans and the whole frightful plethora of junk we had accumulated for the trip, had to be stuffed in rucksacks. And, without fail, we ended up with one rucksack more than we had people to carry them. I could always make myself quite useful up to the end of the packing, but the 'discussions' which followed concerning their porterage normally drove me off to some quiet corner where I could watch the drama from afar. It was Dick, again, who nobly tackled the problem.

(Dick) We had the loads divided up for the porters. Already I counted six packs. Nicas pointed out that we now had only 4 porters, because I'd sent a message that 2 could go down the mountain rather than stay at the inhospitable hut beneath Kibo. Since our four porters had already grabbed a pack each, there was no question of redistributing the contents of the extra 2 packs. There was some bargaining to be done. We tried to buy another porter for the descent, but spare bodies at 15,000 feet were a rare commodity, and they required a hefty incentive. Nicas encouraged one of his friends to join us, which reduced the surplus to one pack. We were wondering about splitting it up and adding it to our own loads when Simon stepped forward and offered to help.

'Thanks very much Simon, but with your big pack already, there's not much you can do really, is there?' Without a word, he whipped out some thick cord and bound two

141

enormous Karrimor Condor 85 rucksacks together, hoisted them in the air and, with a broad grin, he set off swaying down the trail with over 100lb of luggage on his head and the soles flapping off the bottom of his boots.

Once the porters had gone, we attacked our orange plastic plates of muesli, then jammed all the odds and ends in a rucksack, and lifted the bikes for the final ride. The prospect of at least one day's downhill was more than appealing. The slope outside Kibo Hut is sufficiently steep that you just have to sit on the bike, release the brakes and take off. The bikes shot down the slope with us hanging on for dear life.

It was a great novelty to be riding in daylight, and the advantages it afforded over night-time cycling were fundamental: we could see where we were going. This meant that boulders could be ridden round, rather than crashed into. Nevertheless both of us managed to execute horrendous purlers before we were even out of sight of the hut. Dick—always going one better—managed to crash his mountainbike with such force that the handlebars twisted round, the first time we'd managed to make the bikes notice they weren't on tarmac.

The Saddle second time round was one glorious holiday. The sun was shining, the trail was good, the wind was on our backs and we stopped for lots of snaps. The riding was fast and furious, and easy enough for us to drink in the grandness of the scenery.

Kibo the adversary had become Kibo the friend, and in turning our backs to this great mountain we were leaving not a sinister threat to our well-being but an acquaintance who'd been hospitable enough to let us get away with a peculiarly cocky escapade. We should have been grateful.

(Dick's diary, 2 January 1985. En route Kibo Hut—Mandara.) As we were frolicking around on The Saddle, Maggie and Kate should have been finishing their epic run down the mountain. They left Kibo at 5 pm yesterday and aimed to arrive at Marangu Gate before noon today. Maybe they can claim a record! That would be one in the eye for Nick and I! Let's hope they make it down there with no problems (like getting eaten by wild animals!). Today is Wednesday and if the courier is ready to rush the film and words to the Nairobi plane then it should be in London on Thursday with sufficient time to process it for the Sunday Times *this week. John Lovesey has promised to put the I.T. address in the article, so a good report of the success on the summit, and possibly a photo as well, will be our main fund-raising weapon.*

We ricochetted down the trail, jinking the bikes between boulders and jumping steps, racing each other for bottlenecks and running straight through carpets of slippery pebbles that had us sprawling three days earlier. It was wildly exhilarating. The mountainbikes handled like finely balanced slalom skis, kicking up puffs of dust on the turns, swooping down the dips with blue-suited riders hunched low over the handlebars. Goggles kept the flying grit from our eyes, and our red gloves, now holed and ripped, served to preserve skin on the palms of our hands when we crashed to the ground.

All too soon we were closing on the lower slopes of Mawenzi, and climbing the low hill that marks the southern edge of the Saddle. The world of buff cinders and bare gravel dropped behind us and we rolled into a new landscape of living greenery.

(Dick) The sensation was like entering the Land of Milk and Honey. We were coming back to a living breathing world. For three days, we had been above vegetation. Mountain climbers who spend weeks above the snow-line must enjoy a very special sensation when they see fresh plants and running animals for the first time.

We cycled past flowers and grasses, and rounded a hillock to find the muddy oasis of 'Last Water'. Nick cycled straight through the deepest pool, got his wheels bogged and boots covered in mud. I knelt and filled our water bottle.

Things moved quickly again after that. We crossed a gully where we had to carry our bikes, then found the corner where I'd missed the edge a few days earlier. On another slope we had seen the porter with no socks, and further down we found our own tyre tracks. It was like being in a time machine going back over our lives.

Woodsmoke was curling into the fading sky as we crested the rise before Horombo Hut, and the first people we met were a group of porters warming their hands by yellow tongues of flame that were licking up the blackened bulges of an enormous metal cooking pot. So much steam hovered above the cauldron's mouth it wasn't possible to see exactly what was bubbling beneath, but it smelt good. A few trekkers hovered outside huts then ambled towards us. Should we stay the night at Horombo, or press on to Mandara? It was touch and go; dusk was approaching fast, but we were going so well that it seemed a shame to interrupt our downward momentum. We went on.

An hour later we were wondering whether we'd done the right thing. The gullies that had forced us to do so much bike-carrying on the way up the mountain were tricky in the fading light, and now the clouds started rising from the jungle below. Before long we were enveloped in a damp clinging mist which soaked our clothes and turned the path into a greasy mire of mud and stones. Darkness came quickly, and we were forced from the bikes, pushing them down the twisty trail. As we groped our way down, the handlebars and pedals kept catching on ruts and bushes. With a little reluctance, and a lot of moaning we picked up the bikes and settled them onto our shoulders. We were miles from Mandara yet, and it would be a long plod. Our headtorches cut slender furry beams through the water hanging in the air as we stepped carefully on slippery footholds. Falling over here could mean getting a razor-sharp 42-tooth chainring in the jugular.

I was slithering along some way in front of Dick, enjoying the perversity in continuing in such diabolical conditions, yet slightly anxious that we weren't just pushing our luck a bit too far. It's in the closing stages of trips, when you think you're safely home and dry, that rash decisions can be made. We'd already made one: to carry on from Horombo. Only one torch was now giving out a reasonable beam; we had no sleeping bags; no more food, and the trail was treacherously slippery. I didn't want to be the first to suggest dumping the bikes, but if we were to avoid a bivouac in the jungle, it was the only option.

(Dick) The air was chilly and we had on anoraks, yet we sweated inside. We were moving too slowly. My legs were tiring, and my back ached. We couldn't remember how far it might be to the start of the jungle, and how far it was through the jungle to Mandara Hut. Was it one hour? Maybe two?

At 8 pm we decided to cut our losses, and scrambled up into the bushes near the trail and dumped the bikes. In the pitch dark it was impossible to see any landmarks that would help us find the bikes again next day, so I placed a broken tree root on an earthy ridge in the centre of the path. As a back-up, and in case we missed the root in the morning, Nick wanted to count the number of paces from the bikes to the first notable marker. He set off ahead, chanting numbers. Through the darkness, I heard: '. . . 37, 38, 39 . . .' and later '. . . 362, 363 . . .' and, as sleep tugged down on my eyelids and I followed Nick's heels '1,341, 1,342, 1,343. Look, a tree. Remember that!'

We moved much faster after abandoning the bikes. Part of me was annoyed at the separation; part was glad because it meant that we'd have a chance of riding this section in the daylight next day. Dick seemed unashamedly ecstatic to have left them. We came to a parting of the ways, one path veering off to the right, the other continuing level and slightly left.

(Dick) Neither of us could remember which route was the correct one, and after several minutes discussion, Nick set off on his own along the right-hand option. I knew he was wrong, but decided to follow him for up to ten minutes, at which point he'd realise how wrong he was, and have to acknowledge my superiority. For a quarter of a mile I muttered in his wake, and the jungle closed around the trail. Another ten minutes and Nick squirmed down a familiar muddy groove, and we found ourselves on the Mandara track. I was fuming.

Nick went into a hunger frenzy when we arrived at the Hut. He cooked first tea, then soup, then mashed potato, then protoveg stew to go with the mashed potato which had already been eaten. He ate his portions standing up while boiling the next concoction over the petrol stove, staring with mad-scientist bloodshot eyes at his culinary creations. He made more mashed potato to go with the stew that had already been eaten, then made semolina for pudding, with thick powdered milk and jam in lieu of custard. Then more tea, and we crashed out.

We bedded down late after a long day. The reader must not confuse our gallantry and endurance with that of Nicas, Simon and the porters. They had set out from Kibo Hut before us, carrying impressive loads. We had the excitement of a one-off trip; they do this every day. They reached Mandara hours before us, and didn't simply dump our packs, but set to and erected a couple of tents so that we 'intrepid adventurers in darkest Africa' could crawl thankfully to bed.

Soft Landing

Nicas woke us up, a warm enquiring face wanting to know about our crossing of the Saddle and what had happened in the jungle during the night. Dick obliged, with hair-raising tales of cartwheeling crashes and nocturnal blunderings through pitch-black equatorial undergrowth. 'But where are the bikes?' asked Nicas, 'Up there', Dick pointed skywards past the tree-tops to the high flank of Mawenzi, 'We have to go and fetch them now.' Nicas had by now got so used to our odd excursions that he didn't even raise an eyebrow at the idea of our heading back up the mountain.

For the last time, Dick applied his organisational talent to luggage removal:

(Dick) We got the bags packed, and the porters set off on the last two-hour journey down to the Park Gate. One man, Joshua, stayed behind for the last rucksack, a pretty red and white Karrimor Hot Lite which had been subjected to the most awful assortment of filthy unwashed cooking utensils, smoke-black pans and soggy food. We sat in the sun, drinking a final brew of tea, and trying to eat up our last few morsels.

The walk back up through the jungle was a joy. The mud that we'd raved at the night before had hardened in the warm morning air and our legs seemed to power us effortlessly through the trees. In no time we were out on the heathland. Dick spotted his piece of root easily, and, before the astonished eyes of a couple of passing porters, we scampered up into the scrub and pulled two bicycles out of the long grass.

This was the final fling; the last great downhill. We climbed on the bikes, released the brakes, and rocketed off down the narrow track. Dick was leading, juggling his mountainbike through deep runnels only just wide enough to take the bike's pedals. We were going flat-out, not exactly racing each other, but certainly reluctant to let the other take the lead for too long at a time. Overtaking was a problem. Mostly that track was only wide enough for one bike at a time, but there were occasional places where two could squeeze side by side. I hung on Dick's back wheel, waiting for him to make a mistake and give me the chance to slip by. I saw two deep runnels separated by a high mud ridge rushing towards us. Dick chose the right hand runnel; I opted for the top of the high ridge, aiming to accelerate up onto it, overtake while Dick fumbled through the runnel, and pull well clear as I dropped off the far end of the ridge. The first part of the plan worked well: I got the bike up onto the ridge and level with Dick. But then it started leaning leftwards; I tried to correct by tilting my body to the right, but the front wheel inexorably ran closer to the edge then dropped like a stone and I went straight over the 'bars, falling head-first into the ditch. The bike came down on top of me making a large hole in my shin, and I lay completely numb and winded. By the time I'd dragged bike and body from the depths of the ditch, Dick was a speck in the distance.

We paused, hot and sweaty, at Mandara for a drink of water, then pushed off again as the skies opened and a rush of cool rain tickled the leaves on the trees. More mud, but this time it didn't matter. The water beat on our Goretex hoods for ten minutes while we slid downhill on wheels that shot this way and that as they hit patches of oozing ground.

A Frenchman stood on the trail in front of us, laughing. As we drew closer, his hilarity escalated till he was doubled up with either mirth or oxygen depletion. 'Why', he spluttered, 'are you riding bicycles on Kilimanjaro? You must be English. Now I know what I must do next year: carry a refrigerator to the top!'

'What good is a fridge on Kilimanjaro?', I retorted. 'At least you can ride a bicycle, but a fridge would be no help at all . . .'

'Yes, yes, but with my refrigerator I can keep my drinks cool all the way up the mountain!' at which point he tugged his beret down over his eyes and strode off, still laughing.

Steadily we freewheeled down the final leafy miles, sun now lancing through the tall trees. For a few minutes we were in a vacuum, suspended between the adventure that had been and the reality of the outside world that we'd meet once again at Marangu Gate.

'I s'pose,' said Dick, as we bumped along the grass and gravel, 'we've got to think of what to do next . . .'

A small boy, sitting in the shade by a stream, watched two *masungos* deep in excited conversation pedal past on strong black bicycles. They didn't see him, and after they had gone around the bend, he stood, heaved his sack onto his head, and turned towards Kilimanjaro.

Postscript

The £7,500 needed to buy and install the Wajir windpump had been raised by the end of April 1985. Construction started immediately and the windpump should be in operation by September 1985. Further funds have continued to accumulate and it is hoped that a second windpump can be given to a village in Zimbabwe.

Appendix One: Intermediate Technology – the aims, approaches and achievements

I.T. in Action

Intermediate Technology in 1985 celebrated 20 dynamic years of charitable aid. It has grown from the controversial ideas of a small group of workers to become the acknowledged leader in developing self-help projects for underprivileged communities. The spectre of mass starvation and poverty looms over the world and I.T. believes that the effective long-term solution is to help people to work themselves out of poverty. Give a man a fish and you feed him for a day, give him a fishing net and you feed him for life.

Intermediate Technology is still a relatively small organisation, working with limited resources, on the enormous task of helping people in developing countries to become more self-supporting and independent. Every year they receive thousands of requests from all over the world, for assistance in solving technical problems concerned with people's basic needs – food, water, housing, health, agriculture, transport.

Intermediate Technology is committed to the belief that people in the Third World *can* cope effectively on their own, if only they can obtain the small-scale low-cost technologies that are appropriate to their situation. Some examples:

-   A new design of cotton-spinning machine improves quality, increases production and earnings, and uses 25% less power.
-   A small hydro-electric system, developed by Intermediate Technology,

provides power for small industries, and so helps to increase the income of impoverished villages.

- A simple, energy-efficient stove, used increasingly in Nepal, can save at least 30% of a family's previous firewood—a vital contribution to saving the rapidly diminishing forests of the Himalayas.

Good examples of the I.T. method are the fishing boats being developed in Tamil Nadu, India where 40,000 fisherman earn only about £70 a year. I.T. is working with three local boatyards to introduce new, safer boat designs which will increase their catch and therefore their income. These boats are as cheap to produce as the traditional dugout type and hence are affordable by the fishermen. Furthermore they are built from marine plywood which can be made from surplus local wood, rather than the increasingly-scarce huge, old, solid tree trunks. The benefits to the fragile forests of Tamil Nadu are obvious. The new boats will last for several years longer than the dugouts. The most important benefit is that the economy of the boatbuilding yards and fishing industry is rejuvenated and jobs are provided for craftsmen and fishermen.

The energy, skills and determination of the underprivileged are frequently overlooked in Aid programmes. They are the untapped resources which can create a viable local economy. I.T. tries to increase the work opportunities by providing advice as well as tools and equipment which can be made or bought locally. By generating jobs, a community spirit is kindled and poor people gain control of their future and a pride in their lives. Each project is carefully designed to blend with the religion, culture and social fabric of the area. Once a project is established, the I.T. support and advice can be withdrawn and the community becomes self-supporting. It is no longer dependent on finance or gifts from the First World. In this way, I.T. makes a little money go a long way.

Schumacher's Inspiration

When Intermediate Technology was founded twenty years ago by Dr. E. F. Schumacher, author of *Small is Beautiful*, the concept of using intermediate level tools and equipment in projects for developing countries was not considered 'progressive'. Development strategies stressed large-scale, centralised, capital-intensive, labour-saving production: huge factories with impressive automisation and a handful of overseers. This process was, and is, ill-suited to underprivileged countries. In these areas, little infrastructure exists, labour is plentiful (especially in rural areas), and the money needed to buy and maintain equipment is scarce. Typically, foreign expertise needs to be imported to install and service the hardware.

In a village with half the men unemployed, a combine harvester provides work for one and profits for one family. If it breaks down the owner gets foreign help to mend it and must buy fuel to run it. All the village men could share the labour of hand-cutting the crops, share the profits and be independent of outside assistance.

Schumacher realised that traditional tools and methods only allowed subsistence farming or limited production whereas large-scale technologies merely made the rich richer. The mass of the poor and unskilled were therefore excluded from ownership and from benefiting from the development. He realised that what was needed was a technology in between: an 'intermediate technology': something between the tractor and the hoe, between the combine harvester and the sickle. All these work opportunities should maximise the use of local resources and minimise the dependence on imports of materials, expertise and finance.

Schumacher himself was principally an economist. His best-known book expounding his ideas on the appropriate approach to world strategy is *'Small is Beautiful'*. Schumacher's concept of 'smallness' mirrored those of many other writers and philosophers from Morris and Ruskin to Huxley, Rachel Carson, George Orwell and John Kenneth Galbraith. Such eminent figures as Gandhi and Julius Nyerere have also talked about, and campaigned for, such appropriate technologies. Schumacher put it in writing for us all and encapsulated society's concern for its future. I.T. have numerous publications describing the tools and techniques available and the best overview of the state of appropriate technology today is 'The AT Reader' edited by Dr. Marilyn Carr.

Schumacher's ideas came together in the conception of this charity in 1965. Since his death other instigators continue to push I.T. forward and Dennis Frost has now taken the active lead role as Chief Executive. The work is however dependent on the network of I.T. Associates and the voluntary work of countless individuals. I.T. is based at 9 King Street, London WC2E 8HW, though its research and development stations are scattered over England and its Associates all over the world.

The Working Charity

Intermediate Technology was established firstly to locate and ascertain the types of intermediate level tools and equipment which exist and secondly to advise people working in the field of where to get them or how to make them. When gaps are found, and a real need for them to be filled is identified, I.T. undertakes research and development projects in collaboration with local organisations to produce the technology and methods required. They then test it in the field and refine the design to suit the needs, the available materials and the skills of both the people who use, and those who make, the product. The process must always be two way because it is not realistic to develop appropriate tools and equipment without working closely with the people who, in the end, must stake their future on them.

Once a technology or method has been tried, tested and locally accepted, Intermediate Technology looks at ways and means to spread its use as widely as possible. The lessons learned in one area facilitate the introduction elsewhere. In some cases this involves working with government ministries or international aid organisations to create the 'environment' needed for wider dissemination, through changes in policy or promotion through regional programmes.

In nearly all cases, though, the results are published by the charity in the form of buyers' guides to low cost tools and equipment, bibliographies, manuals, case studies, surveys, and technical briefs. Hundreds of titles have been published and distributed throughout the world. Intermediate Technology also publishes two quarterly journals: *Appropriate Technology* and *Waterlines* have subscribers working as volunteers, consultants, missionaries, extension agents, UN experts—even government ministers! Both periodicals act as a forum for those working in the field to share the results—good or bad—of their efforts.

From the beginning, though, Intermediate Technology realised that it alone cannot solve all the problems of the rural poor. The charity has helped to establish similar organisations to help identify and resolve problems on the 'front line'. There are now some 80 appropriate technology institutions worldwide, and it is in partnership with them that I.T. often works, acting as their backup when required.

Projects and Programmes

Intermediate Technology is engaged in a wide variety of projects throughout the developing world, concentrating on food production and processing, small industries, water supplies, transportation, building materials, textiles, rural energy systems, fishing, workshop equipment, and even small scale mining and mineral processing. Always the emphasis is on small-scale, low-cost production and use in rural communities.

Efficient cooking stoves have been developed and introduced in both Indian and African areas. On the Himalayan run of 1983, Adrian and Dick visited one of the Nepalese villages where these improved cooking stoves had been installed. We bent low to step into the mud-brick home and moved cautiously across the dim-lit room to where the lady of the house was cooking. The stove appeared to all intents and purposes to be a standard old clay stove, but this one we were told, had been redesigned by I.T. Most of the work was carried out in Reading, Berkshire. The fire chamber and flue have better airflow and the recesses for pots are in optimum position. The stove burns up to 35% less fuel. This saves trees and wood on the surrounding mountain slopes where deforestation is a problem as it is in most of the world. This saving benefits the women and children who have to collect the wood. The stove is cheap to make, costing only about £1.70p, the same as the traditional types and is made from locally-available clays so that no foreign imports are needed. Furthermore the local potters are taught to build the stoves and hence their jobs remain secure.

A thousand million people lack adequate water supplies for drinking, irrigating crops and for their livestock. The new range of wind powered water pumps to lift water from underground sources should help bring relief. We are hoping to raise enough funds from this *'Bicycles up Kilimanjaro'* project to buy and install a windpump for Wajir. A similar I.T. designed Kijito windpump has been installed in the Turkana area and has made the desert bloom with fields of corn around it. This single pump will last for many years and serves 5,000 people. On other areas it can replace diesel pumps which are costly to buy and run.

In Sri Lanka, where 5,000 village fishermen lost their boats in a hurricane, I.T. has been helping to introduce a new catamaran that can land on the beaches through the dangerous monsoon surf.

Spreading the Load

Intermediate Technology is now the foremost agency of its kind in the world, and the demands for its services have increased enormously. Remaining true to its 'small is beautiful' philosophy, it has sought to maximise its effect while minimizing its size—now 65 full-time people, mostly engineers, economists, and other specialists. If a part of the group has shown that it can generate its own funds, the charity has encouraged its own people to set-up on their own, under the broad umbrella of Intermediate Technology. Today, it is associated, in one way or another, with I.T. Transport, I.T. Power, I.T. Products, I.T. Publications, Development Techniques, I.T. Workshops, I.T. Consultants and the Appropriate Health Resources and Technologies Action Group. In some cases they remain wholly owned subsidiaries of Intermediate Technology but with their own boards of management; in others the charity retains a share holding; others have become independent whilst remaining a part of the extended family. They provide Intermediate Technology with expertise in specialist areas, and in some cases, an income towards its charitable aims. The system is based upon trust, a mutual understanding and common aims.

The Future

The recent famine emergencies have highlighted the urgent need for longer term approaches to preventing such tragedies. In other words the urgent need to provide not only short term relief but also truly lasting relief from poverty. Without such a shift in priorities, the Third World will continue its downward spiral with hundreds of millions facing an even bleaker future than at present. Intermediate Technology has shown that Small is not only Beautiful but also Possible. The challenge we all now face is bringing the benefits of the small-scale, self-reliant approach to the greatest possible number of people.

The Part That You and We Play in this Struggle

Most people who read this book will belong to the richer First World. You will obviously be literate, having had the privilege of schooling, and must have your own finance or useful friends in order to procure this book. At present over 500 million people survive on less than £1 a week. Less than the cost of one night's entertainment.

The most obvious contribution we can make to the world's problem is to give some money to help finance charities such as I.T. Alternatively those of us with specific skills useful to the Third World might wish to offer their services. A wide range of staff are needed: scientists, social workers and administrators. But all research and action require finance. Any fund-raising efforts are eagerly sought. Jumble sales, whist drives and gala nights are all good sources. *'Bicycles up Kilimanjaro'* cost nearly £4,000 from our own pockets but has already generated more than £20,000 for I.T.

The most important contribution we can make is to understand the possible approaches and solutions to the world's problems and to try to inform our friends, relatives, colleagues and the public at large of these concepts. The more people who realise the pitfalls and possibilities of aid, the more progress can be made. Only with a united effort wholeheartedly supported by many many people can we hope to make an inroad of safety for those 500 million people in the sea of poverty.

Appendix Two: The Equipment

The Bikes

Both bikes were stock Saracen ATBs, and the only modifications we made were those to the gearing. The basic specifications on the bikes we took up Kilimanjaro were as follows:

Frame: Reynolds 501 Cromalloy-M All Terrain forks, stays and butted frame tubes. Brazed-on bosses for mudguards, front and rear carriers and two bottle cages. Tange steel headset.

Wheels: Rigida 26″ A.L. 25/32 aluminium rims, laced three-cross, 36 spokes per wheel, on Shimano large-flange aluminium hubs with solid axles.

Tyres: Mitsubishi Canyon Express.

Transmission: Shimano triple chainset fitted with 28-38-48 chainrings; Sun Tour 5-speed freewheel modified by Bike UK to 14-17-22-28-38 teeth: Shimano front and rear derailleurs with steel protector-bar for rear derailleur; Shimano thumb-shifter gear-levers; Shimano bottom-bracket; Sun Tour XC-II pedals.

Gear ratios:

		sprocket size				
		14	17	22	28	38
	28	52.0	42.8	33.1	26.0	19.2
chainwheel	38	70.6	58.1	44.9	35.3	26.0
size	48	89.1	73.4	56.7	44.6	32.8

Brakes: Shimano cantilever; Shimano levers.

Saddle: Brooks B66, leather.

Handlebars: Nitto aluminium.

Accessories: brazed-steel rear carrier; mudguards.

During the ride we made minor modifications: we ditched the mudguards to save a few grammes of weight, and we both fitted frame padding to the tubing to make the bikes less uncomfortable to carry. Bluemels supplied us with a couple of specially-shortened Mountain Range pumps that fitted easily in our rucksacks —where they remained for the entire expedition! There were no malfunctions, nor did we have any punctures during the 8 days on Kilimanjaro. During the Rift Valley work-out we did however manage to snap a chain in half and write off one rear derailleur. We didn't fit toe-clips to the pedals, but there *were* stretches of the ascent where they would have increased the efficiency of the bicycles—generally however, we were falling off too often for toe-clips to be safe. Head-torches proved to be ideal for riding mountainbikes at night because they cast a beam wherever you turn your head—by contrast a conventional bicycle light fitted to the machine will point only forward, and not help you spy out route alternatives slightly to the side.

Once on the mountain, the only adjustments were those carried out on the headsets, bottom brackets and wheel bearings, all of which underwent a natural 'bedding-in' period, and needed a small amount of play taking up after about three days' riding. We also tightened the brake cables before starting the descent.

Modifications we would bear in mind for a future trip would include the following:

1. We'd leave behind mudguards and rear carriers to save weight. All our luggage ended up being carried in rucksacks, on our backs, and taking mudguards up Kilimanjaro is rather like buying suncream for a camel: inessential.

2. Frames with a shorter wheelbase to improve hill-climbing ability. Shortening would worsen down-hill handling characteristics, but on balance the increase in up-hill efficiency would mean it would be worth it.

3. We'd design some custom-made frame padding, contoured to fit shoulders and back, so that the bikes could be carried more comfortably.

4. We'd find two other people to ride the bikes!

Daypacks

Each of us carried a Karrimor Hot Route 55-litre rucksack, containing bivouac sac, food for the day, first aid, suncream, sun/snowgoggles, penknife, the clothes mentioned below plus spare jersey and Goretex overtrousers. We had compass, maps, pen, pencil, diary paper, and an automatic camera. Above the snowline we also carried ice-axe and crampons. Not surprisingly a puncture repair outfit and set of bike tools went everywhere with us.

Pete the Cameraman

Pete had a set of gear identical to ours, minus the bikes and bike tools, but supplemented by a considerable load of photographic equipment. He used Nikon equipment throughout and shouldered at least 20 Kodak films each day in his Karrimor Aventura Professional camera bag. The details of his photographic load are as follows:

Aventura Professional camera bag
2 Nikon FM bodies
1 Nikon FE2 body
1 Nikkor 24 mm lens
1 Nikkor 28 mm lens
1 Nikkor 50 mm lens
1 Tamron SP 70-210 mm zoom
1 Nikkor 135 mm lens
1 Nikon LA 35F auto camera
1 flashgun
70 rolls Kodachrome 64 film
10 rolls Kodachrome 25 film
40 rolls Kodax Tri-X black & white film

Support and Tentage

Michèle, Kate and Maggie had similar clothing to that described above although theirs came from assorted sources. Most of the camping equipment was transported in large Karrimor rucksacks, on the backs or heads of porters.

We had one Black's Wild Country Quasar two-man hoop tent. This was quick and easy to put up. The tent is of integral tension structure so that it can be erected without the need for pegs and then positioned as desired with respect to rocks and tussocks of grass on the ground. We also had the larger domed Super-Nova 3 to 4 man version and this was the tent which we used at 18,500 ft on New Year's Eve.

The Clothes and Load

We both existed on one set of clothing and one small emergency pack each for daytime use. Our support team organised porters to carry tents, most food and sundry items.

Clothes

Berghaus Wengen salopettes with Intermediate Technology teeshirts underneath formed the common denominator of our clothing. These two items, supplemented of course by re-usable underpants, socks and shoes, were admirably suited to the damp sweaty jungle with thick vegetation and frequent crashes. At higher altitudes as the temperature dropped, we added any combination of the Sanctuary Mountain Sports thin thermal long johns, thermal top or the Berghaus Gemini jacket.

The last item was superb. It has an inner Thinsulate jacket zipped to an outer double-skinned Goretex wind/waterproof shell. The outer layer by itself was indispensable in the afternoon rains of the forest. The inner garment was cosy at night. Together, and with drawstrings and cuffs pulled tight, they provided a weatherproof cocoon which was ample insulation up to the worst conditions we experienced at 19,340 feet.

We both carried Helly Hansen balaclavas and Black's thermal gloves at all times, and scarves occasionally. Nick used a conventional woollen jersey for part of both days on the volcanic ridge of Kibo, but Dick seemed to survive merely with his extra layer of fat.

Reebok running shoes with short socks were worn in the Rift Valley, and Brasher boots for all activities below snowline (except sleeping) on the mountain. These boots are light, tough and give good ankle support in addition to excellent traction. On the snows we wore Berghaus Trionic all-leather-upper mountain boots.

Karrimor sleeping bags and Karrimats ensured comfortable nights and the mass of exercise during each day guaranteed sleep. The petrol stoves marketed as Coleman Peak One by Black's gave no problems and heated pans effectively. Although hand-held flat battery torches and headtorches were used for most light at night, we did try to use candles whenever possible.

Dr Mike Townend of Cockermouth, Cumbria, organised a comprehensive medical kit for us. Diamox, the altitude acclimatisation drug was most effective. He also supplied drugs and treatments for traveller's diarrhoea, bacillary dysentery, amoebic dysentery and Giardia. We had bandages, both sticky and crepe, with dressings of a range of sizes, and antiseptic cream. Malaria tablets were essential. Headache pills and painkillers were carried but never used. Most importantly he briefed us extensively on the use of these items and we stowed a handbook on mountain medicine into the load.